NO ESCAPE FROM GROZNY

a christian in war-torn Chechnya

David LeCompte

Front cover carpet element and section separator symbol used by permission – Mr. Raphel Kaffel – Jim Dixon – Don Tuttle: originally seen in "Caucasian Prayer Rugs", published 1998

ISBN 978-1-934932-02-5

Published by Snowfall Press
1832 Woodmoor Drive
Monument, CO 80132
www.snowfallpress.com

Printed in the United States of America

Dedicated to Dottie

My wife and true friend - in life and missions

And to our children Josiah and Elizabeth

We have lived this story together.

Friends along the Way

Helen

Hugo

Bill and Gail

Alan and June

Caleb and Tina

Leo and Maureen

Pastor Brian

Sean

our families...

your friendship through the years has meant so much...

and

Jesus...without you, this story would have never taken place.

Special Thanks

Special thanks to Sean Rafferty for his friendship and professional design on the cover.

No Escape from Grozny

Introduction

I am not a theologian, but I believe God loves all people. I am not a humanitarian aid worker, but I have tried to show compassion in the name of Christ to those who live in hunger and pain in this world.

My journey has led me to touch and be touched by people in the garbage dumps of Mexico City, the lepers and untouchables of India, troubled teens in Russia's Siberian prisons and persecuted saints of China and Iran. I have worked among Kurdish refugees after the earthquakes in Turkey and Armenia, and I have sat in the tents of Kosovo refugees. For the last few years, I have shared bread and lamb with the war ravaged people of the Muslim republic of Chechnya in Russia's Northern Caucasus region.

At the beginning of this journey, I set out to make the world a better place. I am not so sure what difference I have made, but it has been an incredible journey.

There have been those along the way who have encouraged me, and I pray God's blessing upon them. Others have raised their eyebrows and questioned my actions. Some people have a hard time understanding why I would go into war zones to do disaster relief or share the gospel in prisons. After all, living is easy in the United States, and it seems crazy that anyone would want to leave that cocoon.

Yet, when I look at the example of Jesus, I see that He constantly engaged people who lived on the edge of life. He reached out to the sick, the hungry and the wounded, refugees, the outcast, religious prisoners—these were His people.

As a refugee Himself, Jesus knew what it was to be homeless. He was always standing up for those oppressed by political or religious tyranny. He believed so strongly in the freedom of the oppressed that He willingly stood between them and the military might of Rome. His death was not for political purposes, of course, though it seemed that way to some at the time. Jesus knew the politics of His time were just transitory, and that His sacrifice was for a greater purpose, to forgive sin and usher men, women and children into a greater Kingdom.

Like a tapestry, many threads have been woven methodically together to share my experience as a person living out my faith among ethnic Muslims in Chechnya. The events you will read about happened to real people, in real situations, with real consequences. This story takes place in the turbulent times at the end of the 20th century, mostly after the World Trade Center attack on September 11, 2001. It also spans the timeframe of the Northern Ossetian school tragedy in Beslan and the hostage crisis at the Nord-Ost theater in Moscow.

My concerns about patriotism, religious convictions, and moral ethics—as well as my own human struggles with faith and fear—are all interwoven into these pages.

Some threads are darker than others. In some stories, glimpses of hope break through, other times the reality of human tragedy rears its ugly head, and you may laugh, you may cry, or you may even get angry. It is my prayer that, above all, you are moved to action yourself for the cause of Christ.

Chapter 1

A Little Girl Named Nasan

"You are insane to try and create a home for Chechen orphans," the surly Russian soldier said. "We're going to be putting a bullet through their heads in five years."

That was the voice of evil in Chechnya during the nine years I ministered there, trying to create an island of hope in a land so filled with hate and violence that it was said that even the Devil blushed with embarrassment at the atrocities committed there. It was not the only such voice, and at times they seemed to call out from all directions.

I had often rumbled along Chechen streets escorted by armed personnel carriers, protection provided by my hosts, and I would stare out at the grey sky and burned-out buildings, and wonder why God's Spirit had seemed to have departed this place. The capital, Grozny, was like Paris in the minds of the people in this Northern Caucasus region, but it had become nothing more than a sarcophagus with broad avenues. I saw a whirlwind of ashes through the armored vehicle porthole once, and the furtive face of an elderly lady who was out seeking food. I recognized these as icons of the netherworld I was in, a place where corruption was the currency of the land and death was the oxygen that people breathed. I uttered a brief prayer, asking God to spare the old woman from the snipers.

I had not gone to Chechnya because it was the reasonable thing to do. Even those who cared most deeply about me said I must be crazy for my willingness to take the heat of that sin-scorched place.

Of course, reason and sanity had nothing to do with it. The Lord had spoken to me about sharing the Gospel in Chechnya, a Muslim republic in Russia, and all the pros and cons boiled down to a matter of simple obedience to God's will for my life.

And then, of course, there were the children. They were the ones caught in the vortex of madness in the region, where tribal feuds have been raging for millennia, and had been aggravated by Soviet-era interference. Russian president Vladimir Putin wanted to keep the "renegade" Chechen government under his control.

There was suffering for everyone in this parade of malignant regimes, but especially for the children. Up until this point I had only seen their anguished faces in magazines and on the nightly BBC news and I knew I needed to see conditions for myself in Chechnya. It was during my first attempt to get into the war zone that God spoke to me about our future ministry to Chechens. He spoke though a child, and her name was Nasan.

In January, 1997 I embarked, along with my translator, on one of those slow trains that radiate out of Moscow and go to the uttermost parts of Russia. The train rolled on for days until we arrived in Nalchik, the capital of Kharbadino / Balkaria. Although we were still officially in Russia, it was obvious that we had left the land of the Slavic peoples. We now were in the infamous "Kavkaz" region, or as the Russians call it, the "Land of the Chorny Chelovek" or "Land of the Black People."

I had heard that many Chechen refugees had fled into this city during Chechnya's first war in 1994-1996, and I hoped to meet some of them. Upon our arrival my translator and I were introduced to one of the leaders from the local Russian Baptist church, and I shared my desire to visit with some of the Chechen refugees. Although hospitable and friendly, he began to lecture me on the problems and dangers of American Christians befriending Chechens.

"You can visit the refugees here in the sanatorium, but to go into Chechnya and try to help them, well, they will take you hostage or kill you. Since the Russian army has left, all that remains is chaos. They're all Wahhabi Muslims, and you can't trust them," he said sternly.

His words pierced me like a knife— not because what he said was untrue—but because I recognized the situation as something more than mere political infighting. I had felt this before as a child, growing up in Alabama during the civil rights movement. I recognized the evil power of racism and ethnic hatred. It was all part of the darkness of sin to me; not only had I seen it first-hand in the American South, I had also seen it in later years between ethnic Albanians and Serbs in Kosovo, and between Turks and Kurds. Now I felt it again, Russians against Chechens. Same sin, different country.

We visited many Chechen refugees that week. The sanatorium was a huge dormitory that was used to house mentally ill people during the Soviet era. Since the breakup of the Soviet Union, finances had been diverted elsewhere and the building had been left abandoned. Although badly decaying, with no running water or heat, hundreds of refugees from Chechnya had been allowed to take refuge in it.

As I made my way through the building I wondered who was more insane, the former patients, or those who had driven the refugees to this place. At least it was a place away from the war. All sorts of people were there—young and old, strong and feeble, individuals and families—each had experienced the madness of war.

That is where I met a beautiful little eight-year-old girl named Nasan. She stared up at me with black eyes that looked like shiny ebony stones. She was there at the sanatorium with her seven other siblings and her parents. They all shared one small room that had two filthy beds, one for her parents, the other shared in shifts by her brothers and sisters.

There was a rusty hot plate for cooking, one little table, with two chairs, and one bare light bulb that cast stark shadows on the walls. The windows had cardboard and rags stuffed in them to keep out the sub-zero cold. There was a toilet and shower at the end of the hallway. When the toilet worked, ten other families used it as well. The shower was a pipe coming out of the wall and had never worked. Repeated requests to fix it fell on deaf ears. I had seen prison cells like this in Siberia, but those were for criminals, not refugees or little children. I surmised that the authorities had concluded that little girls didn't need showers.

Nasan used to do the same things any normal little eight year-old girl would do—read fairytales, play with dolls, and draw pictures of animals. But all that changed radically one day. Her family lived in a village called Chermin. It was located on the border between Northern Ossetia and Ingushetia, two neighboring republics in Russia's Northern Caucasus region. Northern Ossetia is Russian

Orthodox while Ingushetia is ethnically Islamic, and that was at the root of the cultural differences and the turmoil in the region.

These two neighbors have never been peaceful, their animosity going back a thousand years. In modern times their hatred was contained by the draconian military might of Moscow, but in the fall of 1991, as the Soviet Union began to crumble, the local Muslim leaders in Chermin began to resurrect old territorial disputes, including a claim that land had been taken away from them and given to the Ossetians during the rule of Joseph Stalin. As in many other parts of the former Soviet Union, such disputes were a common occurrence, but trouble here had escalated beyond all reason. This was, after all, the Caucasus, the land of war.

Like a flame fanned by an ill wind, the local militia in Chermin rose up and within days the village saw street protests and organized rallies calling for the retaking of land that was in the possession of Ossestians. Local officials in Vladikavkaz, Northern Ossetia, sounded the alarm to Moscow, and soon Russia's Special Interior troops were rushing south to try and head-off the conflict.

As word of this troop movement reached Chermin, Ingush militia and irregulars attacked the Ossetians. Equipped with small arms and rocket grenade launchers, the Ingush began evicting Ossetians from homes in areas once claimed by the Ingush.

The Northern Ossetian militia responded in force and was backed by Russian attack helicopters and gun-ships. The Ingush were out-gunned and overwhelmed. The battle lasted only forty-two hours, but when the shooting ended, not only had the Russian and Ossetian troops defeated the Ingush, they had pushed the border back even further, making Chermin an Ossetian village.

Most of the little brick homes in Chermin were reduced to rubble. Although Nasan's father was opposed to this uprising, their little home was destroyed anyway. Nasan was now a refugee in a war that she could not comprehend.

Picking up the pieces of their broken home and shattered lives, Nasan's father decided that Chermin was no longer safe and they should go and live with relatives. In a cruel twist of fate it turned out they lived in Grozny, Chechnya, the epicenter of the conflict. Now they found themselves in the sanatorium in Nalchik.

From then on, problems were only compounded for the family. Nasan's father had been disabled by a sniper's bullet in Grozny, and was unable to work to support his family. Because she is Chechen, local employers in Nalchik would not hire Nasan's mother. The only source of income for the family came from small jobs her mother found in the market.

Daily food was bread and soup. Occasionally, when the Red Cross came by with humanitarian relief supplies, there was the luxury of cheese, butter and milk.

After visiting the family, my translator and I turned to leave. Walking down the cold, bare hallway, I was prompted by the Lord to stop and look back. Nasan was framed in the doorway, and she stared at me with her big, round obsidian eyes. I thought about my own children in America who were almost the same age. In that instant I thought about the horrors this little girl had seen and how life shouldn't be such an ugly, fearful thing for her and the tens of thousands of children like her. In that moment, the Lord touched my heart in a new way.

After that experience, the war in Chechnya was more than just images and text for me. I had looked into Nasan's eyes and seen the depths of her innocence and fear. On that trip I had also touched the tear-stained face of a little boy who had lost his parents. I had looked into the haunting eyes of a mother who had witnessed her young daughter being raped by drunken soldiers.

That week I returned to the U.S.A. with a shaken soul. It is hard to describe the uneasiness I felt, for I had seen the results of the raw, rabid attack of religious and ethnic hatred on families, and had seen how it had betrayed and ravaged them. What I experienced that week changed me forever.

Why Chechnya? Why would God choose me to go to such a radical place? I had grown up in Elba, a small Alabama town. My parents were Christians (my dad was a pastor), but I was the black sheep, hanging with the wrong crowd, going to the wrong places, eating and drinking with sinners.

After I became a follower of Christ, it seemed I always ended up going back to those who I felt needed Him most. Could God use a simple, radically changed man from the wrong side of the tracks to reach to the other side of the tracks? Maybe growing up in Elba had something to do with it. Was it because I had French blood in me and we French are known to be a little radical sometimes? Another radical Frenchman named Napoleon had spent time at another place called Elba, and also in the Northern Caucasus, where the Lord was directing me.

The Chechens were the Samaritans of Russia. They were the Kavkaz lot, the black people, the bandits of the Caucasus, rebels and religious outcasts. They were the kind of people that Jesus came and lived and died for, even though in a perpetual war zone. Chechnya was a long way from Elba, Alabama, but maybe not so far after all.

Many Christians believe that once a vision comes from the Lord, that lightening strikes, seas part and the promised land is at hand. This is usually not the case. Visions are more like seeds planted in the soil. In God's timing they germinate and grow, and in due season the harvest comes. That's the way it was for me as I sought a strategy to help the children of Chechnya.

To my knowledge, there were no Christian Non-Government Organizations or (NGOs) working in Chechnya. The thought of my wife and I starting our own organization was a scary proposition both from a logistical and financial standpoint. Dottie and I had been married nearly 15 years as we contemplated starting this new ministry in late 1996, and it was a real step of faith for us.

We had both grown up in Assembly of God homes, and we wanted to serve the Lord. We started out as youth pastors in my wife's home church in Riverside, California, and in a few years we felt God tugging on our hearts to become missionaries. We served with Eastern European Outreach (EEO), and I traveled extensively throughout Eastern Europe and other parts of the world sharing the Gospel.

In 1989 our first child, Josiah, was born, and our daughter, Elizabeth, came along in 1992. As I traveled the world, Dottie kept the home fires burning.

At the end of 1996 we officially left EEO and began our own ministry which we called, In His Fields, to share the gospel in Chechnya.

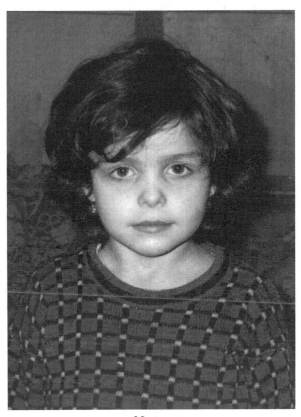

Nasan

Chapter 2

Into the War Zone

It had been three months since I first visited Chechen refugees in the rat infested sanatorium in Nalchik, Balkaria. Not being able cross the Chechen border on my first trip, I was more determined than ever to make it a few months later. In fact, I was so confident that we would get access this time that I brought a team of twelve including volunteers, translators, and a cameraman to document our journey.

Our host organization was a small missionary outreach located in Vladikavkaz, Northern Ossetia. The pastor there had a heart for the Chechen refugees, and in less than 24 hours we crossed the Chechen border with 12 tons of food and clothing for the people of the besieged city of Grozny, Chechnya's capital.

That evening I sat upstairs in their small church. There, alone in the dark, thinking, waiting, praying. I whispered, "God, do you want us to go? Is this worth risking our lives for? Does the world care? Do Christians care?" God didn't speak.

The silence was shattered by a ringing telephone. A contact from inside Chechnya was calling. The person explained that the night before, two Agency France Press correspondents had been taken hostage as they crossed the Chechen border. All that was known was that a "militia group," probably nothing more than opportunistic renegades seeking cash, had taken them and nothing had been heard from them since. The people who were hosting us in Chechnya, their identities unknown to me that the time, were very worried about our safety. Was this God's answer to the prayer I had just lifted up to Him?

Our team waited for another call the next day to confirm whether or not we should proceed with our plans.

That night sleep escaped me as I entertained many doubts and fears. The next morning the telephone rang again. Our host was pleased with the news and shouted to us with joy, "The Minister of Religious Affairs in Chechnya, Abuzar, has made special arrangements for you and the team to visit Grozny and stay at his home." This was a miracle, of course. It seemed to be the confirmation I had been seeking from the Lord.

I learned later that the Minister of Religious Affairs had notified Russia's Ministry of Interior (MDV), the Russian military and the FSB that we were coming. The military had agreed to guarantee our team's safety in and out of Chechnya.

When I found this out, I was perplexed. On one hand, the Russians had the power to keep us safe, but on the other hand it was widely rumored that many of the kidnapping of foreign aid workers that had plagued Chechnya were not being carried out by Chechen bandits, but by Russian FSB agents as a way of keeping world opinion turned against the Chechen resistance. The FSB, of course, continued the surveillance, espionage and "dirty tricks" they did when they were known as the KGB during the Soviet era.

The Russian military unit in Grozny was the Special Purpose Detachment of State Police (called OMON for its acronym in Russian). OMON is a rough and tumble special operations unit, like American SWAT teams perhaps, but with an infinitely worse reputation. They wore black face masks, commonly used excessive violence as part of their daily activities, and were accused of raping and murdering civilians in Chechnya.

I had stressed the importance of traveling under the radar as much as possible to our ministry partners. Our host didn't want to end up on CNN or BBC either, but now, with these new developments, we might as well have sent a press release to the entire region.

The team packed into the gray Russian van that would take us to our Chechen hosts. It was decorated with a red cross on the side and blue light on top. The paint job and lights were not designed to deceive the border guards, only to make it less obvious to bandits and renegade mercenaries that a load of foreigners was coming to town.

This wasn't my first choice of transportation, of course. I recalled that it was exactly the same type of vehicle that American philanthropist Fred Cuny was using as cover when he was trying to broker a peace agreement between the Russians and Chechens under the auspices of the Soros Foundation in 1995. The ruse didn't work, and he disappeared. His bloody passport emerged, but his body has yet to be found.

Like slimy sardines in a can, we bumped across the Republic of Northern Ossetia and Ingushetia toward the Chechen border. Eight military checkpoints later we arrived there. It was 1:45 p.m.; fifteen minutes early, at least by western standards, of the time we had agreed to meet the officials from the Ministry of Religious Affairs.

I surveyed the situation with trepidation. I am a person of faith, but at the same time, waves of uncontrollable paranoia were flooding my mind. There was no delegation there to meet us. No guards, nobody, except for some rag-tag militiamen who eyeballed our van with suspicion. Were these the same guys that had taken the French journalists hostage two days before? Were they the ones who had made the phone call to us? Was it all a set-up? We dared not get out. Where were the people from the Ministry of Religious Affairs?

Suddenly, out of nowhere, a military jeep and four other vehicles sped up the road. They pulled alongside our van and came to a halt in a swirling cloud of dust. Robust men in Gucci suits, Ray-Ban sunglasses and American military fatigues stepped out of the vehicles, each armed, some with Kalashnikov automatic machine guns. They didn't look very religious to me. In fact, they looked more like Chechen rebels and Russian mafia than mullahs. We're cooked, I thought. We'll be taken hostage just like the correspondents.

Instead they politely greeted us, " *A Salaam Alekum*" ("Peace be to you") and identified themselves as representatives from the Ministry of Religious Affairs. They apologized for being late to meet us; they had to wait for a Russian OMON tank detail to detonate a mine in the road coming out of Grozny. Welcome to Chechnya.

Within minutes our team was transferred from our Russian sardine can into four Chechen vehicles. The two trucks carrying the humanitarian aid followed us into Grozny. Speeding away with reckless abandon, we weaved our way through the maze of massive craters and potholes created by the barrage of rockets and Grad missiles that Russia had unleashed upon this tiny republic.

Some of the craters were large enough for a car to disappear in, and sadly many had. Tree tops shredded by the unrelenting wave of Hellfire rockets from helicopter gun ships lined the road leading from the Ingushetia/Chechen border to the outskirts of Grozny. Devastation stretched as far as the eye could see.

Scattered among the gently rolling landscape, typical Caucasian brick farmhouses lay broken and crumbling. Huge holes blown into their walls from tank and artillery fire, a vivid example of "mouse holing," a military tactic used to prevent guerilla fighters from ambushing columns of tanks from within houses. The roofs were smashed by mortar fire, windows shattered by shrapnel and bullets.

Boxcars and oil transport cars had been blown off their tracks. They lay strangely scattered, upside down, in fields, in creek beds, in courtyards, like parched dinosaur bones, baking in the hot sun. The black fields, farmland much like rich soil of upper Michigan, was dormant, not from neglect, but from the contamination of landmines. The air was black, a result of the hundreds of oil fires still burning.

What troubled me most were the dozens of twisted, charred automobile frames that littered the roadsides. They were fiery memorials to the thousands of refugee families who had been mercilessly slaughtered trying to flee along the "humanitarian corridor" that Russia's military had guaranteed. The true story had been revealed later that the guarantee was only a cruel propaganda ploy to lure Chechens onto the roadways where Russian helicopters and gun-ships could easily slaughter them with Hellfire rockets and heavy caliber machine guns. Just like America's Cherokee holocaust, this was Chechnya's "Trail of Tears," stretching from Grozny to Nazran. "The road of blood" our driver grunted.

As we approached Grozny, one of the armed men in our jeep started shooting into the air, stopping traffic so our convoy could pass through without stopping. There wasn't any electricity in the entire republic. Not that it would have mattered because there weren't any signal lights either. No street lights, no electric poles—everything had been bombed flat.

I would later learn why the Chechens always drive fast and frantic. It is more for security reasons than show. The logic is simple; it is harder to hit a fast moving target than a slow one. I guess it goes back into the Northern Caucasus history as well, when most of these people were rugged mountain horsemen. Wild and untamed, they still had a flare for risk. The speed could have also been a device to dodge the bullets they fired into the air. Gravitational laws ruling, bullets shot into the air come down somewhere.

We entered Grozny from the south through the infamous Minutka Square. A series of sixteen-story apartment buildings had been reduced to rubble by Russian aircraft rockets and heavy artillery. Burned out hulls of concrete, shredded metal and steel now entombed thousands of Russian and Chechen civilians buried beneath. A year had passed since the last survivor had been pulled from the debris. Most would never be found—their bones and blood had become one with the soil.

Near the Central Bazaar, in downtown Grozny, dozens of young Chechen men manned their little wooden stalls selling everything from rocket-propelled grenades (RPGs) to anti-tank machine guns. A new AK-47 machine gun could be purchased for under $100.

The burned out hulls of T-72 Russian tanks were monuments to the lives of the many Russian and Chechen fighters who had done battle here just a few months earlier. Our driver commented proudly that the streets were much cleaner than they had been just a few weeks prior to our visit. I couldn't imagine what it must have been like to live in this inferno during the height of the fighting.

Our motorcade maneuvered quickly through the cluttered pathways that doubled for streets in downtown Grozny. The tata-tat-tat of the AK-47's repeated at every intersection. Block after block, the evidence of the death and destruction that had taken place in this city was screaming from the very ground.

People on the street stared with puzzled looks on their faces, wondering what all the fuss was about. Was someone important passing by? Surely, no VIP would come to Grozny, not this place, not this God-forsaken place. We drove on to the home of the Minister of Religious Affairs.

We came to an unassuming residence surrounded by a brick wall. Our host, Abuzar, came out to greet us.

There were several others there as well—city officials, family members, and a funny old man from Kazakhstan There were also servants—lots of servants.

Our team moved through a small arched gate into a large courtyard. Abuzar invited us to sit down and relax in the shade under a large porch. Two Chechen ladies brought cool drinking water and towels to wash our hands. Slippers were provided for our feet, and taking off my hot and sweaty shoes was a great comfort. The last few hours had been a frantic blitz. I didn't realize how much emotional pressure I had been under. For the first time in two days I felt like I really could let down. Taking a cool glass of water, I closed my eyes for a moment and my mind shut down.

As I rested, the little old man from Kazakhstan came and sat down beside me. He patted me politely on the knee and in a masterful display of linguistic ability he proudly poked his chest out and in a heavy broken accent he spoke the only English words he knew, "Zit don peas."

Startled, I didn't quite know how to respond to him. I said, "Nice to meet you" and "I am already sitting down, thank you."

He burst out laughing, not at me, but, I think because he was surprised that I had understood his broken English. He was an odd old man, but you could sense he was excited to meet an American. He reached up, touched the Aussie hat I was wearing and smiled really big. Some things are universal. He didn't have to know English to let me know that he liked it.

We had just begun to settle in when there was a loud knock at the gate. Abuzars' guards scrambled to investigate the source. They greeted a small group of men who had come asking for Abuzar and the American team. In the group was a very distinguished man in a suit, and it was obvious that our host knew him. After a few minutes of discussion the man walked back out of the gate and returned with a TV cameraman in tow. Lights! Camera! Action!

As it turned out, this man was the "Wolf Blitzer" of the local TV station. He had heard of our visit and wanted to interview me to learn why Christians would come to Chechnya.

In my heart I was petrified at the prospect of Christians being on the six o'clock news in Grozny, but evidently this was God's doings and He had a plan. It began to sink in that, other than this opportunity, there was no way we could share our faith with the entire Chechen population in one night. We had planned to remain low profile, deliver food and look for ways to share the Gospel. Now, our efforts had turned into a full blown media event with the entire city of Grozny watching us on TV.

After introducing us as a "Mercy Mission" from America, the man conducting the interview asked what our purpose was for coming to Grozny. This was the door I had prayed for—the opportunity to tell the Chechen people about God's love.

Inwardly, I prayed for boldness, and then opened my mouth. Like water flowing forth, the Lord gave me the words to proclaim His message of salvation to the Chechen people.

"We are believers in Jesus from America," I said. "We want the Chechen people to know that God hasn't forsaken them. We are here to proclaim His message of hope and grace. He will restore your life if you trust in Christ Jesus the Savior of the World."

My translator looked at me like I had just dropped a nuclear bomb—I had.

Followers of Jesus had come to Chechnya proclaiming that Jesus, the good prophet of the *Koran*, was the Savior of the world! How would that go down with the Muslim population?

The interviewer thanked us for our time and wished us well in our endeavor. Abuzar sat silent. I could tell he was weighing the words I had just shared.

As the ladies prepared dinner, a young servant led us into the house to wash our faces and hands. Entering the room used for greeting guests, an old black and white TV was broadcasting a special meeting being held at the Kremlin in Moscow between Russian president Boris Yeltsin and the Chechen rebel Aslan Maskhadov.

With a sigh and apology, the man turned the rabbit ear antenna to try and get a better reception. "Before the war we always got great reception, now we are lucky to have this TV and can watch something," he said.

It was surreal to be in Chechnya watching these two men boldly declare the fighting in Chechnya had ended, and Yeltsin said that General Alexander Lebed had been appointed to negotiate a peaceful transition for Chechnya's total independence from Russia over the next five years.

The Chechen guards listened to every word. Everyone wanted to know what would happen in the future. Some believed what they were hearing, some scoffed. "We've heard this before," they said. Faint gunfire could be heard in the distance from where we were sitting. So much for speeches and declarations.

Nightfall brought the cooler evening air and gave a welcomed break from the heat of the day. By this time the long porch had been transformed into a feasting place with a long table in the middle filled with food. Our host's family joined our team and security guards—lots of guards, 17 in all. There were more guards than guests.

In a corner of the porch there was a large cooking stove where two Chechen ladies were laboring over large pots of food. They had prepared enough to feed an army—at least a small militia. Fresh vegetables, home made meat pies, fresh oven bread, meats and soup. The table couldn't hold anything else.

One of the main food dishes was chicken and dumplings. I wondered how they had acquired my Southern Alabama grandmother's recipe. In traveling the world, one thing I have learned, a chicken is a chicken. No matter if you are in Russia or Argentina, God has designed the chicken to be a life-sustaining source of food. Food is universal and basically the same, just prepared differently. Tonight it was prepared southern style.

There is another thing I have learned in my travels. The guest is expected to eat until it makes him sick, not quite literally, but I have been close many times. There are no ways around it. The host is offended and feels that you're not happy with his hospitality unless you eat large amounts.

Offending the host and the cooks was the least of worries for one of our young team members. Her problem was not gaining weight, but young soldiers. During the hour and a half at dinner, she received five marriage proposals from the young men in Abuzar's militia.

Having survived the love feast and with the marriage proposals over, we sat around the table as baklava and tea were served. It was now time for conversation.

Abuzar's tone turned somber as he began sharing his feelings about the war and the current situation inside the Republic. The hardships and horrors that were continuing to plague the people were becoming unbearable. Chechnya had become a nightmare for those who were trapped there.

Fighting back tears, he related stories of tragedy, heartbreak and human suffering for over two hours. Bombings, killings, children losing their mothers, mothers losing their children, everyone had lost something or someone dear.

" *In sha la*— this is Allah's will," he said. It was awful, and I cried.

Although he had listened to the TV interview, Abuzar was still puzzled why our team had come to Chechnya. He wanted to know if what I said was really the truth and did I believe that God had not forsaken the Chechen people.

After hearing his stories it seemed too simple to just tell him to trust in Jesus Christ and everything would get better. There was no guarantee that would happen in Chechnya during this time of political and military turmoil. In fact, from a material and physical standpoint, it might be fatal for people to profess Christ at this time. After being on the evening news, we could be martyrs for Christ in this land.

The evening was fading fast. Abuzar and I agreed to continue our discussion the next day. Even the little old man from Kazakhstan was yawning. Yet, before going into the house to settle down for the night, he shuffled by my table and poured me one more cup of green tea.

With a twinkle in his eye and a smile on his face he leaned over and softly said "Zit don peas."

The Chechen guards at the table smiled and nodded in respect to the elder man. It was a fitting way to end the evening. Everyone was absolutely exhausted. Every fiber of my body and mind was spent. Running on adrenaline for days in the high risk atmosphere had taken everything out of me.

The security guards had prepared several rooms for our team to sleep in. Closing my eyes that night I reflected back on the events of the day, the week, the past months. Six months prior to this trip I was trying to decide what direction to take in life. Now, I was lying on my back wondering how I had ended up in Chechnya. It was too much to contemplate at the moment and tomorrow's schedule was full with meetings.

I had just drifted off to sleep when suddenly the silence of the night was shattered by gunfire. The young guards were quick to reassure us it was only local militia's warning others about driving into their territory.

We all settled back down and tried to sleep, but how could we sleep?

Russian Soldier's Memorial – Grozny

Chapter 3

No Escape

It seemed like only minutes until the alarm clock went off—a red and white rooster crowing outside Abuzar's house. "Not yet," I thought. Grabbing the sheet I pulled it back over my head.

The smell of food was drifting across the courtyard. Rise and shine! Bacon, eggs, and pancakes on the griddle. Well, not quite. Bacon wouldn't have gone over well with Muslims.

I closed my eyes again and began clicking my heels together. Nothing happened! "There's no place like home! There's no place like home!" I repeated. A compartment of my mind answered back. "I'm afraid not Dorothy, you're no longer in Kansas. In fact, you're nowhere near Kansas!"

I slowly opened my eyes, stared at the ceiling, and tried to re-enter the surreal world to which we had come. No one else was stirring, except for the ladies outside on the porch cooking breakfast. Good morning Chechnya!

The security guards were sound asleep. I was glad we hadn't needed them during the night. Maybe we had needed them and they had been awake all night watching over us. I would have never known. I think we could have slept through a gunfight. Maybe we did.

Rubbing the sleep from my eyes I sat up and tried to focus. My face felt like it had been beaten and my skin was tight. Sleep had been deep and hard.

Looking into the old TV we had watched the night before, my reflection stared back like a distorted circus mirror. That confirmed it; I looked as bad as I felt.

Looking closer, the surreal feeling of being here during a war came into view once again. There, taped to the top of the TV, was a figurine of Woody from "Toy Story" staring straight down at me.

First it was the chicken and dumplings, now it was Woody.

Was there a conspiracy going on here? How did they know that "Toy Story" was one of my favorite movies? My childhood sub-conscience immediately kicked in and I dared Woody to a western showdown.

"Reach for the sky," I snarled.

A member of our team saw what was happening and growled back, "Somebody poisoned the waterhole."

It seemed we all were having mental breakdowns.

Everyone, including our security guards, was awake by now. Our team broke out into hysterical laugher at the showdown.

The security guards looked at each other as if questioning our sanity. Then they caught on to our little game and laughed as well.

It was a great way to break the ice on a new day in Chechnya. There was enough sorrow and pain to feel depressed about. The Bible says, "*A merry heart doeth good like a medicine.*" Sometimes, a good laugh can be the best therapy for a wounded soul. I wondered what caused Jesus to laugh when he walked the earth. We all needed a good laugh that morning.

Outside, the courtyard was already alive with the ladies getting the breakfast ready. Sitting at the long table were a few of the security guards who were cleaning their AK-47's and talking with some in our group. One particular young soldier had taken an interest in a music boom-box our group had brought. A trade was in the making, one boom-box for one Kalashnikov automatic rifle.

It was a tempting proposition but they couldn't come to an agreement that getting caught trying to get it in through U.S. customs was worth going to jail over. Fortunately, the deal fell through and both were disappointed.

Gathering on the porch for breakfast, the little man from Kazakhstan greeted us with his big smile and the now familiar, "Zit don peas."

The young soldiers joined us, renewing their efforts to negotiate a marriage deal with one of our young ladies again, and yes, once again, that deal fell through.

The table was filled with food. Breads and jams with hot tea and fruit was plentiful. With the hardships of war, I was surprised to see so much food available. I had heard of the hospitality of this place but now I was seeing it firsthand. Whatever they had, they would share. This was my first experience with their culture and lifestyle. I took to it quickly.

We had a busy schedule with many places to visit. We had 12 tons of food to deliver and logistically this was no small task.

Abuzar came out and briefed us on the agenda for the day. He had a worried look on his face as he informed us we would have to leave early that afternoon. Intelligence sources had informed him that we would not be safe to stay another night at his house or in the Republic. It seems that many people had seen the interview on TV the previous night and word had reached the FSB that not everyone was happy about our presence. We were on borrowed time.

We had scheduled three meetings for the day. First, we would visit a children's home in the center of the city, then we would go to Hospital #5, Grozny's main pediatric ward. Finally, we would join the Russian Baptist Church in a afternoon communion service.

It would take a miracle to complete all of these stops, but we were going to try. With engines roaring, lights flashing, and yes, automatic weapons firing, we headed out.

At our first stop we visited a lady named Assa. She had taken in thirty-five orphan children into her three-room apartment.

It was heartbreaking to see these kids cramped into such a small place. The air was thick and stale, the bunk beds simple. It was safe, however, and better than the basements where they were living before.

For Chechens, this situation was beyond embarrassment. Abuzar hung his head in shame as Assa shared her disgust with the war, the plight of the children and the lack of government support to help them. The children stared silently at the walls while Assa went on and on.

To get to the next appointment, we had to pull ourselves away from the children in Assa's apartment. I wondered if she and the children felt like a sideshow in a circus where people come in and stare, take pictures, get a few stories and then go back to raise millions of dollars, only to see minimal help actually return. I didn't want to be like that. God helping us we wouldn't be like that. We would help no matter what the cost.

Just around the corner, Hospital #5 was the only pediatric ward in Chechnya. There, skilled doctors lamented the fact that they couldn't operate efficiently for lack of medicines to treat even minor sicknesses. Even so, they persevered during the fighting by hooking up light bulbs to car batteries to provide care for the most critical patients. As professionals, they spoke in disdain, embarrassed to admit they were under such barbaric and humble methods.

What they lacked in facilities they had made up for in courage, saving who they could. Reluctantly, almost apologetically, they showed us what used to be a very well equipped facility. Now it was stripped clean, except for the bloodstains of the past. The stains were everywhere, embedded terrors, echoing under our footsteps as we walked the dark hallways.

Room after room was filled with lives touched by violence. One little girl had her left arm mangled from shrapnel. A young boy, playing with what he thought was a harmless toy, lost his hands in an instant when the mortar exploded. A teenage boy was racked with pain—a misguided step, the sharp click of a pin, in a fateful instant his foot disappeared.

There were some older people in the hospital too. There was the elderly lady, eyes burnt white by the searing heat flash of a rocket. She shouldn't have watched, but like she said, "I just couldn't believe what was happening and went outside to scold the soldiers for committing such crimes against innocent people like me."

She would never see again. Maybe it was better that she didn't, for her world had been destroyed.

Down the hallway was the makeshift maternity ward. There, several tiny babies were being cared for by a solitary nurse in a white uniform and tall blue hat.

She was silent as she went about her work, gently touching the babies giving them assurance and comfort. She was the only mother they had now. Their real mothers had not made it. Some had lost their lives in childbirth, some after, but either way, because of the brutality of war, newborn children would never know their mothers.

One particular little baby was isolated in a corner and tied down in its crib. Born prematurely during one of the rocket barrages, it gasped for air, now aided by an archaic apparatus that looked more like an old vacuum cleaner than a sterile respirator. The baby would surely die. Maybe God would be merciful and take it quickly.

I didn't want to see anymore. Who in their right mind would? Chechnya was dealing with situations where right minds were a luxury, not the norm.

We left soon thereafter, but not before taking a photo with the doctors. They had insisted. As we stood on the front steps for the photo, we could see the large group of Chechen women and children, all victims of tragedy, who had gathered in the courtyard for treatment. One of the doctors said in a pathetic sigh, "They need us to help them, but with what, band-aids and aspirin? We need antibiotics and surgical supplies."

The gravity of the moment didn't have time to sink in—it was all too numbing.

Our next stop was the Russian Baptist church. Even though it was not Sunday, a special meeting had been scheduled by Abuzar and the Pastor, a gentle man named Alexi.

By the time we had arrived the elderly congregation had already begun to sing. We were greeted at the door by Pastor Alexi and his deacon, and we then proceeded into the sanctuary.

As I walked onto the platform where the pulpit was, several militiamen followed me. I thought that this was radical. I have been in some very unique church settings before, including dark hotel rooms in China, Friday night prayer services in Tehran, formal

Armenian worship services, and secret Bible studies in Kurdish areas and the Arab quarter in Old Jerusalem, just to mention a few. However, this was the first time I have ever been actually guarded by soldiers sitting behind me in the choir loft while I preached. I guess there is a first for everything.

The congregation was mostly elderly Russian ladies, their heads covered in typical orthodox fashion for Babushkas, although it also is part of the conservative Russian Baptist tradition.

The contrast between our two groups revealed the two worlds from which we had come. Add the third element of Abuzar and his Chechen militia, and the scene could have come straight out of a Star Wars movie.

Nevertheless, the time we shared together in that church was incredible. Before leaving, Pastor Alexi took me downstairs into the basement. There I saw the place where their congregation had huddled through the worst parts of the bombing. The walls were cracked and had structural damage. Abuzar believed their prayers had saved the church building. In fact, it was the only building in the Octoberskya district of Grozny that was still standing.

After a brief time of fellowship with the congregation we had to be on our way. Leaving the church, all of the members came out and stood along the road, blowing kisses and waving goodbye as we pulled away. They had only met us hours before, but they treated us like they had known us forever.

Although it was not on our original schedule, Pastor Alexi insisted we visit a nursing home before leaving. It was not a pleasant place—a State sponsored home to take care of pensioners and invalids.

Destitute and forgotten, emaciated frames of human flesh lay in soiled beds in tiny rooms, lonely and sad. The stale odor of unwashed flesh hung like a cloud in the air. Auschwitz and the concentration camps of WWII came to mind. I had experienced similar situations in the Gulags of Siberia, but this was worse. The only difference between the home and Auschwitz was there weren't any guards or barbed wire. It was not a fitting place for those blessed old souls.

The nursing home workers began crying and begged us for help. They complained that the Russian State Emergency Services had not supplied any food in over two months. Soup and bread was all they had, and they were running out of that.

The workers themselves had not been paid and some were hungry and some were sick. It was an awful situation. Even our Chechen guards hung their heads and cursed. What kind of evil beast would treat their own people like this?

A couple of years after our visit, the famous, and now deceased Russian journalist Anna Politskoskaya, would write about the barbaric treatment that befell these precious old people in her book, *A Little Corner of Hell*. The Russian film, Dom Durukov or "House of Fools" was also based upon a similar home that was unjustifiably bombed during the war.

Embarrassed and wanting to avoid further humiliation, Abuzar reminded us that the sun was getting low and the border would be closing soon. We had to leave immediately. No more time for ministry, no more time for interviews. The jeeps were waiting. The militiamen and security guards began to move us into our vehicles. Abuzar and Alexi would stay, only the guards and drivers would accompany us back.

With lights flashing, horns blowing, and automatic weapons firing, we sped off towards the border. Just like we entered Grozny, we left—as a spectacle.

We became like tumbleweeds as the emotional whirlwind of life once again gained momentum. We had been sucked into this incredible black hole of war and horror called Chechnya. Spinning, twisting, turning, it had consumed us. We` had been taken hostage by it, but now, it was spitting me and the team out, and we were trying to make sense of it all. We were leaving in one piece. One piece physically, I mean—none of us would ever be the same emotionally.

The border was just ahead, and Chechnya and Grozny were behind. The drivers of the jeep and cars raced wildly, playing tag, to see who could get to the border first. I'm not sure who won because it didn't matter to me. I was suffering from emotional and spiritual overload after seeing so much suffering.

I reflected on the fact that our host and the pastor had to remain. It was my first encounter with these people, and while I felt a special bond with them, there was little I could do for them. I wish we would have had more time to say "goodbye and God bless you"—as it was, I felt as if we had been torn away from these new friends. We were leaving, they would stay. They had to. They didn't have a choice.

As for me, I was leaving, but the people of Chechnya had captured my heart that day. There would be no escape from Grozny.

Grozny – Prophetic warning

Chapter 4

An April Fool

It was late January 2000, and I had just returned from visiting Chechen refugees in the UN camps of Ingushetia. I had been unable to get back across the border into Chechnya for over 2 ½ years because of the renewed war and the security issues that were part of the conflict. Anyone traveling in Chechnya at that point in history would have had a target around their neck.

During this time, God was preparing me for further work in Chechnya, but I traveled to other areas in the Middle East sharing my faith in Christ as part of the In His Fields mission, all the time praying for the right time to return. That time was about to come.

The phone rang in our IHF office in Pennsylvania and the long distance echoes told me it was not from anywhere near.

"I understand that you have 15,000 copies of the Chechen Gospels of Luke sitting in a warehouse in Moscow" said the voice on the other end of the line.

"Who is this?" I asked.

"My name is Geoff. I am a captain in the Salvation Army (SA) living in Rostov, Russia. My family and I manage a project in Chechnya providing baby food to Chechen mothers and refugee families. We would like to include one of these Chechen Gospels with each package. We hear you and your organization have a heart to reach the Chechens for Christ. Would you be willing to donate some of these to us?"

"We will donate every single gospel under one small condition. That I am able to join your teams inside Chechnya and participate in the distribution," I said.

Without hesitation Geoff was happy to accommodate my wish. "No problem. We would love to have you join in. The next team will be delivering two trucks of food in April. If you want to join the SA team, I will arrange it and introduce you to our manager, Idris. Idris and his people will take good care of you. You can trust them with your life. Blessings and see you soon."

The phone went silent.

When our organization first became involved in Chechnya, one of our top priorities was getting God's word into their language. Through the efforts of a Swedish organization called IBT, translation on some portions of the scriptures had been done and more was being worked on. The first Gospel translated was Luke. It had been completed in the summer of 1998 and one of IBT's representatives had challenged IHF to print 15,000 copies. It wasn't printing them that posed the problem. It was distributing them.

Having just survived two years of war and devastation, Chechnya was ripe again for trouble. The political vacuum left after Russia's military retreated in 1996 was filled quickly by the radical branch of Islam known as Wahhabism.

Men like Basayev and Khattab influenced the people. Although Aslan Mashkadov had been freely elected president, he couldn't control the powerful mullahs who ruled from within. Sharia law was implemented and the situation for many Christians, Chechen or non-Chechen, became extremely dangerous.

So, the question then was, if we printed these Gospels, who would distribute them? We didn't know at the time, but we printed them anyway.

Once the printing was completed, we stored them in another mission organizations warehouse in Moscow. Except for a hundred or so that we had the opportunity to distribute through indigenous Chechen believers that had fled Chechnya and were living in other Northern Caucasus cities, the remainder of the Gospels stayed in storage for over a year and a half.

Now, despite Russian president Vladimir Putin's new war to totally wipe out all Chechen rebels, God was giving us the open door to put His Word into their hands. I rejoiced that I would finally be able to share God's word in person with the Chechen people; a request that I had been praying about for years was coming to pass.

I called our travel agent and booked a ticket to Russia on March 28. I then called my good friend Bill who had been a team member on our initial trip to Grozny in 1997. "Hey Bill, want to be a real fool this April 1st?"

Bill and I were met in Vladikavkaz by a young Russian couple who had lived and worked at the Baptist Church in Grozny.

After the Wahhabism gained power in the late nineties, they were forced to flee Grozny and had been living in Northern Ossetia. They had heard of our plans to go with the SA team and wanted to join the humanitarian aid caravan to see what was left of their apartment and the Baptist Church in Grozny.

The SA team would take two large Kamas trucks of baby food from their warehouse in Nazran, Ingushetia to Komsomolskaya, a small village outside of Grozny.

We had brought IHF funds to purchase food in the markets of Vladikavkaz, pack them into two smaller trucks and then meet Geoff and Idris at the Chermin border crossing. It would be vital to have them there to clear us and these two smaller trucks.

I called the number Geoff had given me a month earlier. Hearing his voice was a comfort. "Be at the Chermin crossing tomorrow morning, 9 o'clock," Geoff said. "Idris and I will meet you."

Weeks before, the 15,000 copies of the Chechen Gospel of Luke had been transported down to the Nazran office by a SA truck from Moscow. It seemed ironic that today baby food and God's Word would be joined together. One, saving life, the other, saving the soul, both desperately needed.

The constant turmoil of war had created myriad neurological problems for many new mothers and newborns. Compounding this situation was the fact that fresh baby formula and vitamin supplements were not accessible to most because of closed borders and the dangers of travel. The infant mortality rate had skyrocketed.

Waking very early the next morning I slipped into the kitchen of the apartment where we had slept that night. After hot tea, cheese, and bread, we prayed and prepared to leave for the border to meet Geoff and Idris.

The small trucks had been loaded the night before. Now we needed open doors to accomplish our plans. Looking out the window through the narrow spaces between the many rows of Soviet apartment buildings I could see the first light of dawn radiating off of the snow covered peaks of the Northern Caucasus mountains to the south. I thought about David's words in the Psalms. " *I will lift mine eyes up to the mountains. That's where my help comes.*" I looked to the mountains that morning.

Our two trucks dodged potholes and morning traffic as we made our way toward the border of Northern Ossetia and Ingushetia.

The checkpoint at the little village of Chermin lay just ahead. Coming closer I could see the long line of cars already waiting to cross into Ingushetia. Men stood puffing cigarettes and nervously pacing back and forth hoping for mercy from the OMON guards. Women and children walked hand in hand past barbed wire and concrete and guns and tanks, all commonplace things in daily life in a region at war.

There are several infamous border crossings in the Northern Caucasus region. Chermin is one of them. Usually the length of time you spent waiting was in direct connection with the amount of money you were willing to bribe the officers with.

Having acquired special papers from the SA in Nazran, we were able to move right to the front of the line of people. This didn't mean that we would actually get cleared, it only meant we would enter the interrogation process faster. I had navigated this border many times and it never was a pleasurable experience.

The sign wired to the iron bar read "STOP" in English. Some things are a paradox.

The rugged face of the Northern Ossetian border guard peered into our window. "Documents," he grunted, no please or thank you added.

After handing over our passports and papers we waited, and waited. Then we waited some more.

You could see across the border into Ingushetia. There, other people were waiting for friends, relatives or business partners to return from Northern Ossetia. Although there is great distrust and enmity between these two ethnic groups, business is business.

A small Mitsubishi van pulled up and two men got out. I made out the SA shield that could be seen faintly on the side of the vehicle. This must be Geoff and Idris. But how would they know we were sitting at the checkpoint on the Northern Ossetia side? They had never met us and we didn't have any markings on our trucks.

I watched intently hoping one of them would be able to clear the Ingushetia side and come through the "No Man's Land" between the borders. This would allow them to come over and meet us and help us process our paperwork. We continued to wait.

Our trucks never made it out of Northern Ossetia. We were allowed to cross the border and proceed on to Ingushetia on foot, but the two trucks and their drivers would have to wait for a special piece of paper before they could cross because of the food we were transporting. This piece of paper could only be acquired through a customs office back in Vladikavkaz for a small fee, a price invented on the spot to augment poor salaries. The trucks would catch up to us at the SA office in Nazran. For now, we would travel on.

Bill and I walked over to the Ingushetia side and there we were greeted by Idris and Geoff. Although we couldn't identify them, they had no problem recognizing us. Our shoes gave us away. We were the only ones without the signature black pointed shoes that most Ingush men wear.

Geoff was bright-eyed and warm. An Irishman, he sported a reddish beard which made him look the part of a rebel fighter, except for his Salvation Army jacket.

Idris, a Chechen, was clean shaven and in a suit. He was outgoing and confident. He was the "fixer" as they say. He jived with the border guards, letting them know that he knew how to play their game and win, and most of the time he won.

Their driver was a small, older man named Said. He was a teacher by trade, but since there were no schools left operating in Chechnya at the time, he was doing whatever he could to earn a living.

The little Mitsubishi turned away from Chermin and headed into Nazran. We would stay at the SA office until our two trucks rejoined us, and then the entire convoy would head into Chechnya, hopefully by late that afternoon.

Late afternoon came, and so did our two trucks. Joining with the two larger Kamaz trucks our convoy was now ready to go into Chechnya. We only had a couple of hours to get across the Chechen border and to Gikalo, the village where Idris lived, and where we would spend the night.

Idris brought Bill and me into his office before leaving. "I understand that you are Christians and that you want to help our people," Idris said. "I believe in God but maybe not the same way you do. Many of the Chechen people claim to be Muslims. Most are not. They may be religious but that's all they are, just religious. We are happy that God has sent you to help the Chechen people. We are in a horrible situation right now. Our souls are being ripped out by the war. Please do not be afraid to go into Chechnya. God will be our security. No harm will come to you if God wills. We will have security guards to protect you. May He prosper us in all we do."

After two long years of waiting, I was returning to the war torn land of Chechnya. God had opened a door of opportunity to impact people's lives with His hope and grace.

It was heartbreaking to know that Chechnya was once again gasping for life after the recent military bombardment under the iron fist of Russia's president, Vladimir Putin. Unleashing its brutal military fury upon the tiny Republic in the fall of 1999, Putin had promised to wipe out all rebels from Chechnya, "Even if we have to chase and kill them while they are in the toilet", he had declared. Now, as a result of "Putins War," Chechnya's second war in less than ten years, what had not been destroyed in the first war of the Yeltsin era now lay smoldering in rubble and ashes.

Russia continued to pound the mountain strongholds of rebel leaders Mahskadov's and Busayev's fighters with artillery and rocket barrages. Helicopter gun ships were on constant patrol strafing anything that resembled enemy activity, real or imagined.

At night, Chechen fighters played cat-and-mouse guerilla warfare tactics by raiding checkpoints and outposts and then disappearing back into the night.

Suicide bombs were also used by the "black widows," Chechen women who had lost husbands in the fighting would take revenge on Russian soldiers by placing bombs on their bodies, then stand in line to cross a Russian post or checkpoint detonating their bombs and themselves at the optimum time.

Chechnya was still one of the most dangerous places on earth. In fact, according to the U.N. report on places most polluted with land mines, Chechnya ranked number one in 2002.

The thing that always bothered me the most about Chechnya was not the war, but its reputation as the "Kidnapping Capital of the

World." In the ten years of the recent war, scores of journalist, humanitarian aid workers and a few Christians had been either killed or taken hostage in this volatile region.

A few high profile cases had made the international news including Fred Cuny of the Soros Foundation and Anna Politskovskaya, journalist for Nova Gazetta in Moscow. Some Christian missionaries had been taken hostage and released in nearby Dagestan. Most had never been heard about. I didn't want to be added to either list.

It was late afternoon when we pulled out of Nazran. Idris led the caravan in the little white Mitsubishi with Bill and I sitting in the back with two armed guards riding shotgun in front. The two small trucks were next, the larger Kamaz trucks following them, and then another armed jeep escort bringing up the rear. The large trucks were filled with baby food, formula, and most importantly, the Gospels of Luke.

The main road into Grozny from Nazran is called the M29. Its main border post between Ingushetia and Chechnya is called the Kavkaz post. Like Chermin, it too has an infamous reputation for being less than favorable. Now with the war, it had gone from bad to almost impossible to get across unless you had special friends in the government or special clearance from the Russian military. Chechnya at this time was officially closed to all journalists, aid workers or foreigners, except us. Why we were allowed in I will never know.

In the distance of less than twenty one miles from the Kavkaz post to the turn-off that went south of Grozny towards Gikalo I counted 17 OMON checkpoints. At each post we would have to stop and allow the guards to look into the trucks and inspect them for weapons.

Idris would talk to the soldiers and assure them we were doing Christian humanitarian work in Grozny.

"Chechens? Christian?" they laughed. "Chechens can't be Christian, Chechens are Muslims! We are Christians! We are Russian!"

Not once at those checkpoints was my passport taken. I was being transported into a new world, the land of no passports.

It was late evening when we pulled into Gikalo, Idris' rural village. The dirt streets were shared by cows, chickens and cars alike. Our van stopped in front of the home of Arbi and Miriam. Simple and hospitable, they had the largest house in the village, and that night we would stay with them.

A man of small stature came out and opened the large green gate allowing our vehicle to pull into the courtyard.

"I am Morat," he said. Please come in, handing us slippers for our feet. Morat was a kind little man with a rugged and scared face.

Idris later told us that Morat was an orphan as a child; his father and mother died in the Chechen deportation of Kazakhstan in 1948. Idris had found him in 1996 in a jail in Nazran after the first Chechen war. Rotting away without anyone to care for him, he probably would have died from the beatings and the alcohol he was consuming. Idris had allowed him to come and live with them, part caretaker, mainly servant.

Morat was happy. He also was a brave man in that he had stayed in Gikalo during the latest fighting, forbidding soldiers from ransacking Idris' home. Morat also cooked the best chicken and onions dish you would ever want to eat.

Arbi greeted us and welcomed Bill and me to Gikalo. Dinner was already on the table as we walked inside. Lamb, potatoes, fresh onions, bread, and of course garlic, had been prepared for us. We ate until our stomachs were full. It had been a long stressful day, and as dinner ended I was looking forward to quiet sleep.

We were taken to a large room where we would sleep that night. It was totally empty of furniture, just a large open room with two windows on the side. They had wide masking tape stretched across them—not because they were painting, but to keep the glass from falling in on us in case of shelling. Not that it would really help but it was reassuring that they had tried to protect us in that way.

Bill grabbed a blanket and was in one corner, I took the other corner. Our Russian friends and translators from the Baptist church were bedded down on the other side of the room. It was dark—very, very dark—the kind of dark that makes the hair on the back of your neck stand up. There wasn't any electricity either and the batteries in my little mag-lite were dead too. Best thing to do was just to find the blanket, curl up on the little mattress and go to sleep.

I could hear artillery and rocket fire exploding in the night in the nearby mountains. It didn't matter at this point. I was so tired, I was asleep within minutes.

April 1, 2000 arrived. No fooling. On this day in America, I knew people were playing tricks on each other. But there was no lightheartedness here. In the night I had felt panic grip me. It seemed like little demons were darting in and out of the heavy atmosphere that surrounded us. The gray tones and heavy fog added to the mysteriousness of our mission. Were we fools to come to this spiritual stronghold? Who did we think we were to come and try and liberate it?

On this day we would travel into Grozny to distribute the food we brought and visit the same House of Prayer Baptist Church we had visited before. It would be an emotional day.

We left Gikalo the same way we had entered the evening before. Back up into the city through the same checkpoints. The border guards all knew Idris. The benefit of working through local contacts was obvious.

The fog moved in and out of the crumpled, shelled-out buildings that used to stand proudly along Grozny's Leninsky Boulevard, the main drag through town.

Nervous eyes from roof-top vantage points followed us as we weaved our way through checkpoint after checkpoint.

The constant stop and go caused our convoy to progress slowly, much slower than Idris or Hizir liked. Our drivers were anxious. The faces of our security guards grew tight. We were in the region known as Ockobriskaya Segment, an extremely dangerous area—sniper alley—Grozny style.

We had prayed before leaving the house, and I sensed God's presence with us. However, I did feel some anxiety, and it was hard to hide it. One of our guards said, "I hope your God doesn't mind tanks and guns. He wouldn't like it here. Doesn't your Bible say that God guards you with His angels?"

By God's grace, we finally came to the street the church was on. Stopping short, the driver took one look and then put the van in park. One of the guards had gone ahead and motioned for us to walk down the street. I would not have driven down there either. Burned out car frames, fragments of houses and brick lay scattered everywhere. There was also the possibility that the church property could have been booby trapped with IED's. This was Chechnya, and nothing was sacred.

Idris led the way and soon we came to what was once the Baptist church, its burned out walls black from the hellish fire that had destroyed it.

Taken too was the pulpit where I had stood three years earlier, encouraging the believers to keep the faith through the midst of turmoil and war. Gone too was Pastor Alexi, a martyr beheaded by Wahhabi extremists.

We had heard that Abuzar had been kidnapped by mafia thugs looking for money. The Chechen guards that sat in the choir loft that day while I preached—they too were gone. Everything was gone. Only ashes and memories remained.

My mind went back to all the elderly saints who had been in that church service that day. Where were they? Had they all died in "Putin's War," as it is now called?

Walking back out to the street we turned to look one last time. The heartache was unbearable. God's House of Prayer had been reduced to rubble.

I remembered the first visit, the congregation testifying of God's miracles and how He spared the church during the first war. I remembered as they waved good-bye and threw kisses in the air in gratitude. This time there was no waving, only silent steps as we departed. No kisses, only tears, for this time God did not spare the church building. Did He spare any of the people? Only eternity would tell.

It was a somber moment as we walked back to the van, but there was no time for crying—we had to move ahead. We had two huge trucks filled with food and we needed to drive into the center of the city where we would distribute food near a relief compound run by the Russian Emergency Services.

Several Russian Armored Personnel Carriers (APCs) and their guards were assigned to provide much needed security. I would come to appreciate this arrangement.

I was shocked as we pulled into the compound. I had seen photos of concentration camps in WWII, but I was not ready for this. Chechen men, women and children stood in long lines waiting for a cup of soup and a piece of bread. The horrors of war and hopelessness were etched into their sunken faces, their eyes glazed over from exhaustion and mental torment.

We were not prepared for what was about to happen. People were in such a dire need of food, that, as we arrived, a small riot erupted, trapping us and our trucks behind a wall of surging Chechen women. They were frantically pushing and shoving to get whatever they could. It was both terrifying and pitiful. Dignified women, dark lines under their eyes from sleeplessness, humiliated beings, desperately clawed their way toward the trucks like little children, begging, grasping, pleading for anything that could help keep them and their children alive.

Idris and his workers from the SA were trying hard to process documents and register the ladies in a prompt manner in order for them to receive a food parcel, but this necessary procedure took time.

Some of the women began to panic thinking they were not going to get food. That started a domino effect, and we lost control of the situation.

Our security guards pushed us back into our vehicles to protect us from the mob of women pushing against the truck. Automatic gunfire erupted into the air from the security guards trying to regain control. It didn't matter to these women; they felt dead already. We had brought food and they needed it. Our only option was to drive the trucks out onto the street and away from them to re-establish a new perimeter.

Our driver pulled away with several ladies still hanging to the sides. Some had crawled into the back, and we almost ran over one woman and her little girl as we sped out of the square and onto the street. The women followed, running down the street after our trucks like starved cattle chasing bales of hay in the winter. It ripped my heart out. Under his breath Idris was cursing the war.

Our bodyguards were embarrassed at the indignity of the moment. Bill and I felt overwhelmed. We stopped a quarter of a mile down the main boulevard but the women soon caught up and the jostling started again. We handed out food and Bibles as quickly as we could.

Before nightfall our little team had distributed over 1000 food parcels and Gospels of Luke in the downtown streets of Grozny. Our presence had created such a riotous situation that officials recommended that we leave before dark to avoid more problems.

The war in Chechnya was over as far as major military events were concerned. Civil unrest was still raging. Over 200,000 people remained homeless or listed as IDPs—Internally Displaced Persons. Thousands had fled to Ingushetia and were living with relatives, or worse, in the U.N. refugee camps of Sputnik or Karabulak.

The Russian Army continued to do *zacheetkas* (cleansings of Chechen villages). Many of those who had fled the villages would not return for fear of being extorted, wrongfully imprisoned or killed.

Bill and I had come to Chechnya for several reasons. We wanted to build a relationship with Idris and his SA team. We also wanted to see the Gospels of Luke put into the hands of the Chechen people.

Also, I wanted to see how we could best help children. The image of eight year-old Nasan standing in the doorway at the sanatorium was something I could not escape. I knew I had to do something. During this visit I was praying the Lord would give me insight about what would help most.

There was a lot of danger in the visit, but a lot of blessing too as we accomplished these goals.

I can remember those who told me I shouldn't go. "You are a fool for going there," they said. How fitting, because the apostle Paul also endured such talk. Like him, we were not ashamed to be April Fools for Christ.

Old Woman-Russian Orthodox Church-Grozny

Distributing Bibles and baby food

Mother and daughter - Grozny

David & Bill – Russian Baptist Church – Grozny

Chapter 5

Christmas In Hell

"Pack your bags. The trucks of Christmas packages are finally here, we are going to Grozny," Idris yelled up from the hotel lobby.

I had returned home from Chechnya after the near-riot we had caused in April, unsure if humanitarian projects in Chechnya were wise. In late August I received a phone call from Geoff Ryan sharing that in September, the Salvation Army's humanitarian project in Chechnya would close. Idris and his workers would be out of work.

I traveled back to Nazran in early September to meet with Idris. During this time he challenged me and IHF to organize a special outreach to supply much needed winter clothing and supplies to the orphan children in Grozny. He would organize the logistics and IHF could come and deliver the packages personally.

I prayed for direction. It came as hundreds of IHF supporters and Christian volunteers in America helped purchase, package, and ship over 2500 individual Christmas gifts for the orphans of Chechnya. January 2001 would be a pivotal time for IHF's future work in Chechnya.

Waiting for the shipment to arrive, our small team had been stuck in the infamous Assa Hotel in Nazran. Once a vibrant, semi-western quality hotel, constructed during the oil boom that gripped the Ingushetia government after the Soviet Union collapsed, the Assa was constructed to accommodate foreign oil workers and their families.

Built by Turkish businessmen, the three story structure glistened in the sunlight against the Northern Caucasus Mountains. Well dressed Ingush ladies welcomed you in perfect English and with western courtesies. Security guards, remote control gates, a restaurant and bar, Internet, satellite TV, hot water, the Assa Hotel was "the place" in town—until war broke out in Chechnya. Now the only guests were war journalists and NGO workers from Europe. Reporters from the BBC, AFP, Reuters, CNN, all came to cover the war in Chechnya, albeit from the sanctuary of the Assa Hotel. Putin had declared Chechnya off limits to journalists and observers from the outside world. The U.N., *Medicines san Frontiers* (Doctor's without Borders), International Committee of Red Cross (ICRC)—they came too, but their work was limited to the refugee camps of Ingushetia.

I had stayed at the Assa Hotel several times and each time it gave me the creeps. Eyes seemed to peer out from every cracked wall. The Ingush FSB kept close watch on everyone, especially foreigners. After all, there was a war going on next door. Whether war journalist, humanitarian aid workers, arms dealers, narcotics or human traffickers, every foreigner was there for a specific reason. Our reason was about to be realized as our Christmas packages for war orphans had arrived. It was good to leave the Assa Hotel and Nazran behind.

The cold January air knifed through the car as we joined the convoy of trucks on the jammed M29 road heading toward Grozny, the same familiar route I had taken many times before. At the Kavkaz checkpoint we picked up a Russian military escort—an APC carrier— its crew nursing a couple of bottles of cheap vodka, which they considered human anti-freeze. One of the soldiers joked and asked, "Why are you Americans going to Grozny? Don't you know you will be spending Christmas in Hell?"

The afternoon turned cold and gray as a light snow began to fall. The winter white somehow helped mask the ugly scars of war that blighted the landscape as we passed Samaski, Achoi Martan, Batumi, and the road leading to Vedeno in the mountains, each village carrying horrible memories of massacres. Chechen women stood by the road, some holding babies wrapped like Mexican burritos in blankets, some in bright colored winter clothes and high-heeled boots, waiting in the snow for packed mini-buses to take them somewhere—anywhere.

Five young Chechen boys walked along the road selling home-refined petrol and cigarettes, their faces dirty with soot from kerosene fires they burned to keep warm. Idris stopped and bought some cigarettes from them. One boy wore a knit cap with the L.A. Lakers logo on it—in black and silver, a pirated copy. He didn't care, it was warm.

Our trucks rolled slowly towards the next checkpoint. Two OMON guards left their guard shack and walked over to inspect our documents and trucks. After a few moments of chit-chat and the exchange of a few rubles, our vehicles pulled forward and began the familiar snake like weave through the final barriers of the maze.

Back onto the road, staring us in the face, was a huge, crudely painted sign with the words "Welcome to Hell" written in large red letters in English. The words of the soldier at the border hit me like a cold slap in the face. I realized that it was January 7, 2001, Russian Orthodox Christmas Day. His remark made sense—we were going to Hell on Christmas Day!

The evening drifted into night as our vehicles stopped in front of a little house located in the center of Grozny. We would sleep that night in one of the most dangerous cities in the world. The APC was parked between the two *Kamaz* trucks to protect the Christmas packages from thieves.

We hoped to hide the fact that aid had arrived in the city and foreigners had come with it. We didn't want to start another riot like the last time.

There was no electricity in the city. For lights, we had torches that burned as open flames. Shadows from the flames flickered like fiery ghosts on the walls. I sat in the little courtyard with one of the Russian guards named Sasha. He was in his late teens and his hair cropped short, U.S. Marine-type. Small lines like arrows were cut into the sides of his hair just above his ears. He noticed that I was looking at these. "Those are for each rebel I kill," he said. His sniper rifle, night-scope attached, was leaning against the wall within arms reach. He was *Speznat* —Russian Special Forces. He stared silently into the flames.

Joining the IHF team on this special outreach was Helen Thompson. Helen and I worked together at EEO from 1992 to 1996, the years of prison ministry in Russia. Her grandparents and ancestors came to America from the Caucasus region. She was raised in California by her immigrant parents and she spoke fluent Russian and knew the culture very well. During an IHF trip to Kosovo in 1999, we both sensed the Lord leading her to become part of IHF's work. Her gift of translation would be vital, but her ministry as a woman among the women and children in Chechnya was even more important. After prayer and blessing from her husband Ken, Helen was returning to the land of her ancestors.

Helen became an integral part of IHF's work as our ministry grew in Chechnya. Far beyond just translating, Helen poured her life into the people there. Whether witnessing to a Russian soldier, embracing a fearful mom-to-be in a bombed out maternity ward or sharing Bibles stories with Chechen orphans, Helen shared God's love with all. Continuing to live with her family in California, she traveled extensively, managed IHF's west coast office, and coordinated IHF's ministry to share Christ in one of the most dangerous areas of the world. She was a Godly and brave woman.

Months of hard work had gone into organizing this special Christmas outreach. Packing, shipping, waiting—it all was in God's hands now. Today we would become the arms and feet of thousands of Christians in America who had given of their time, money, and efforts to see a Chechen child receive God's love through their gift of clothes and Bibles.

It was bitter cold in the street. Hell had frozen over. We pulled on every stitch of clothes we had as we prepared to move once again. The APC carrier belched black diesel smoke as it struggled to start in the sub-zero temperatures. Finally, with a rattle of cold steel pistons, the motor fired. Our soldiers scrambled to climb aboard the icy killing machine for another ramble through the dangerous streets of Grozny.

Our trip would be short as we sped through the streets to Stadipromoslovskaya region on the north side of town. This region was the hardest hit and every home had either been destroyed or severely damaged. Idris knew the mayor and recommended that we conduct our distribution in that district since it had suffered so much. The administration posted an announcement the day before that anyone with children should come to the office of the mayor the next morning at nine thirty to receive a special Christmas gift from the "Friends from America"

Our trucks turned onto the street of the mayor's office. Men, women, children stretched in a line for at least three city blocks. Some stood by wood fires built for warmth.

"Many have stood in the cold for over four hours waiting for you," exclaimed one of the mayor's assistants.

There were hundreds of them, maybe a thousand, and more were coming. I panicked. "Idris, we only have 2859 packages!"

Idris chuckled. "What should I do, send them home? Don't worry, this is Chechnya, we are used to this. Some will have to share."

As our trucks pulled into the compound, the mass of people began to surge forward. My mind raced back to April the previous year. This can't be happening again, I thought. You could see the expressions on their faces begin to change as anticipation and hope of receiving something gave them life, even if they didn't have a clue about what they were going to receive. Someone had brought something for them, and that's all that mattered.

The mayor was named Adam, and he invited us into his makeshift office and greeted us with warm hands and a warm smile.

"I apologize for the conditions of our office. I know it is a little cold in here. I hope we can warm you with our gratitude. Thank you for coming to our region, we will do all we can to make you safe. Who are you and why have you come?"

Helen and I shared with Adam that our organization IHF represented many Christians in America who cared about the fate of the Chechen people. And, because they cared, they wanted to share with them the hope and love of Jesus in a practical way—Christmas presents for the children in Grozny.

Adam sighed deeply and said, "We are Muslims, you are Christians. Our children don't need our religions. They need shoes and food. But if your Jesus wants to risk coming to this place and give our children shoes and food, then He is most certainly welcomed."

With trucks in position, the security guards had created a human corridor for the people to receive packages. Funneling them into a narrow opening that led to the back of the truck, control was established and the package distribution began.

I hoped we had enough packages.

Before leaving Adam's office to distribute some Christmas gifts, our team was invited to eat a small lunch they had prepared. As most of the building was bombed out, the small lunchroom was exposed to the cold. We all sat down at a wooden table with our jackets and gloves on. You could see our breath.

In a crude field kitchen, two ladies were working over a hot stove. They had prepared *galushki*, garlic bullion and flour dumplings. They served it in plastic bowls and it smelled good. However, it was so cold that the piping hot soup began to congeal and grease over before I could even begin eating it. Trying to eat soup with gloves on is not easy either. We were so cold that each of us began to laugh at the other. Our teeth began to chatter and our knees knocked together. Adam saw what was happening and he also began to laugh. Nobody could eat but we all were having a great laugh while we froze to death. Seeing our plight, Adam left the room and returned a moment later with a clear bottle.

"Friends, I know Christians don't usually drink alcohol. But today, I will not be the one responsible for your freezing to death in Grozny. Please, in honor of Christmas, let's toast this day of your coming to help our children!" As he poured about 100 milligrams into each of our glasses, we all braced for the shock.

" *Nastaroviya!*" We each turned our glass up, and down the hatch it went. It was immediately apparent that this was far beyond the standard forty-proof vodka. We had downed what we the good ole boys down in Alabama used to call "White Lightning." Pure alcohol. The kind you can run an automobile on. Idris called it *Benzin* or Chechen airplane fuel. Helen's eyes were wild and wide. Idris and Adam were grinning from ear to ear. From head to toe, my entire body began to feel warm. We would not freeze that day.

The package distribution went well. The contents were awesome. Wrapped in pretty, bright paper, the sweaters, boots, gloves, school supplies, hats and a few luxury items brought joy to the faces and lives of each recipient. What were the luxuries that caring Christians had included? Candies, a racing car for the boys, hair products for the girls, each a precious item to a child in a war-torn world.

Some people in the U.S. had included a photo of their family, some wrote small letters. The most important thing in the package was the wordless bracelets, telling the Gospel story. Combined with a small Bible booklet, every package was a living testimony to the saving grace of Jesus Christ and His love for Chechen people.

Adam watched as Helen and I and other team members interacted with some of the women and children. One little 12 year-old girl named Fatima clung to her grandmother's skirt as they walked up to the back of the truck.

"Her favorite color is pink," the grandmother said.

Her mother brutally killed, Fatima was shy and withdrawn. She looked at everyone suspiciously. She cowered in fear seeing the guards with guns. They reminded her of the horror of what had happened that awful night. Drunken soldiers, marauding through their home with reckless hate and passion had used and abused her mother as she watched. They discarded her like a worthless animal when they finished, then turned on Fatima. Sweet little Fatima lost her mother and her innocence that night.

Slowly, Fatima's face began to light up with joy as she opened her package that afternoon. It was filled with a white and pink sweater, pink winter gloves, white wool socks, a doll, school supplies, and a pink hand-knitted cap. Christmas had come to Fatima.

She asked about the wordless bracelet and the Bible booklets. Helen shared with her the message of hope and that Jesus Christ loved her and would never leave her alone in this world. She listened to how she could have joy and peace with God and that He loved her so much. Fatima seemed to grasp the message as she began to smile and move without clinging to her grandmother, who was crying by now. Helen was also crying. Even the war hardened soldiers were moved. I stood by Idris and Adam, strong Chechen men. They were silent. God was speaking.

David and Russian Special Forces – Christmas 2001

Grozny

Christmas Package Distribution

Women Wait for Christmas Packages – Grozny

Little Fatima

Chapter 6

The Fish House

It was early June 2001. Spring had returned to Chechnya and trees were budding and the green grass had replaced the grays of winter. Wild flowers dotted the landscape adding color to otherwise dreary conditions.

I had returned several times trying to make a decision about where to go from here. Should we continue to conduct short term outreaches or we should we commit ourselves to a longer more permanent work?

If more permanent work, what would the nature of the work be?

Where was help needed the most? Was it in the refugee camps in Ingushetia or should we go straight to the heart of the problem, the children within Chechnya who were in the center of harms way?

In a way, the decision had been made long ago, but I knew it was not one I could force. I had to patiently wait for the Lord to put the pieces together, and I was seeing that now. It was time for action. We would start a home for orphaned children.

Idris and his wife Maleka had been a great help throughout the January project. They needed work and we needed a local family that would work with us. They said they would be happy to manage a children's home. He had done this type of work before with a United Nations project after the 1994-1996 war. They became our family and we became theirs. Now we needed to find a place to begin the work. But where?

On previous trips, Idris and I were meeting with officials from Grozny that were offering buildings and help, but the city locations were bad for many reasons. The children didn't need to be exposed to that place anymore. They needed a place to live a normal life. Now, once more, we drove out of Grozny and back down the dirt roads towards Gikalo, Idris and Maleka's village.

Turning off the main road into their village, cows and chickens wandered lazily across the roads. Sheep and goats grazed on tender shoots of grass poking through the snow and mud in front of the ragged gates of the little rural homes. I thought to myself, this is the place. We should start here, in this village—a true, indigenous community where we can make a real difference, one child, one life at a time.

After some thought, Idris and Maleka suggested a large building in the village that had once been used as a day-care center. It was huge and would take enormous amounts of money to renovate it into usable shape. Even so, eager to do something, I looked at the property and made a proposal to those who controlled it.

After a few meetings, the owners asked us to consider renting the property with the option to buy it in five years. They also made the explicit requirement that we not conduct any religious or Christian activities at the property. Of course, I could never agree to that. How could I? We were disappointed.

Sitting in the small room of their house, we shared our disappointment and frustration. There must be something else we could find in this little community. Just then, Idris thought of a man in the village that wanted to sell his house and move back to the mountains where he was from.

Idris reminded me that this was the same man we had taken some presents to on an earlier visit to their village. He was taking care of his niece who was disabled from MS, and we had taken them some flour and sugar on an earlier trip. We immediately jumped into the car and drove to his house.

It was late afternoon as our car bounced down the muddy road in the village. Splashing in and out of mud holes, it felt like we were riding a horse instead of driving a car. The mood of failure was fading and the gray cast sky was giving way to splashes of sunlight. I felt excitement again.

The house was on the outer road of the village with a large field across the street. As our car rolled up to the gate my eyes fixed on the two story house in front of me. It looked like all of the other houses in the village—except for something very unusual.

The brick masons that had built this house had done something very strange for a Chechen community. Under the windows of the house they had carved the shapes of fish in the bricks. Not just under one window, but under every window were bricks carved like fish.

I am not one to put much faith in signs, but I felt this was no coincidence. Stepping out of the car, I pointed out this unusual feature.

Idris said,, "Isn't that your symbol?" referring to the Christian sign of a fish. I looked at him and smiled. Was this also a sign that a Muslim was asking this?

We knocked on the green gate. Opening slowly, we were greeted by Liza, the young girl. She smiled bashfully and invited us in.

Walking through the gate, I sensed a peaceful feeling. The inner yard was an open space where sheep, chickens, and other animals were roaming freely. There they were, young sheep grazing on the grass, peaceful and contented, unaffected by our presence and the turmoil going on around them. I pinched myself. Was this another sign? I was beginning to believe.

We walked to a shelter where the elderly man was sitting. Standing to greet us, he leaned against the trunk of a huge grape vine that ran out over a large arbor at the back of the house. Almost four inches in diameter, it had been growing there a long time, shading and providing fruit for those who received it from its branches. Now, would it bear fruit of another kind? I was almost convinced.

Although by now I was sure that all these signs were God's way of showing me that this was the place, I was not prepared for what happened next. As Idris and I sat down with the man to negotiate, I realized that I had not properly introduced myself to him. Apologizing I asked his forgiveness and introduced myself as David, or *Daud*, as the Chechens called me.

Acknowledging me, he kindly accepted my apology and said "My Name is Isa, (Jesus as it is translated in Chechen and Arabic) and I wish you good success with your work here."

This was enough for me. We settled on a price and bought the house from Jesus that afternoon.

The house where Isa lived is where we would start a home for Chechen orphans. The brick carved like fish was a sign of the physical substance that the children would know as they lived in the home. The sheep grazing was a sign that all who entered this home would find peace, warmth and a true pasture for nurture. The grape vine was a symbol of the joy that would be found in the home. And most important of all, these signs were types and shadows of

Jesus the owner—how fitting it was for him to be living there all along!

Now that we had secured the place to begin our work, there was one last hurdle. I had to obtain permission for the work from Kiem, the head Islamic leader in the village. Without this we would not have been able to operate. I had met him before, but this meeting was crucial. I began to pray and perspire.

A soft spoken man in his late seventies, Kiem invited Idris and I into his home. Sitting cross-legged and wearing the traditional *papaka* hat, he welcomed us into a large room. The floor was covered in ancient Caucasus carpets, and tapestries on the walls were embroidered with verses from the *Koran*. The ladies of the house brought in hot tea and sweets from the kitchen, giving our meeting official status. Greeting us, he asked our welfare and purpose for visiting.

I went straight to the point. "Kiem, you know that I have come to Chechnya many times. You also know that I am a Christian and follower of Isa. Christians care about the war orphans here and we want to open a home to care for them. I am asking for your permission to do this."

Kiem looked down at the floor for a moment and then, looking up at me he said, "Daud, you and your friends from America are most welcome to come to our village. For years now we have suffered and struggled to survive this war. None of our Muslim brothers have lifted their little finger to come and help our children. They are hypocrites. You are most welcome here!"

Within days, the men in the village started new renovations and construction on what we decided to call Lamb's Home, a place for Chechen orphans and needy children.

Since we needed to be ready for the coming school year, a deadline of September 6th was set for completion by Idris and Maleka. I thought they were crazy considering that we needed to build so much and had so little time to do it. The whole project seemed crazy, and I thought it would be a miracle if it happened. If Jesus had worked miracles in the past, then he definitely needed to perform another one here. After all, this was His house.

The next day I left for the United States, but I returned a month later to check on the construction progress. The house was in total renovation mode, and the foundations for the new bui dings were poured. New bricks were already forming the walls. I was shocked! In all, there were over twenty-two workers on the site. It was a hive of activity. The village was buzzing with talk about Isa's house being transformed into a home for orphans.

The workers themselves were special, all local tradesmen. The men were busy laying the bricks and installing the windows. The women were the plaster and whitewash artists. I say artist because they really were. Their specialty was plaster coating the interior walls. The most interesting part of their work was watching them mix the crude mud and straw coat that preceded the final plaster.

Using centuries old methods similar to adobe brick making, the ladies would pour clay mud and water into a large metal vat, then stepping into the vat with their bare feet they would begin to blend the mixture like they were stomping grapes. Little by little they would add fine straw to the mix and slowly it became a strong and workable material.

Then, with strong graceful sweeps, a short, stocky woman would apply the mixture onto the ceiling and walls, smoothing it to perfection. After this layer dried, a finish coat of whitewashed plaster was applied, finishing the process.

The project was progressing nicely. The walls were going up and the roof would go on soon. The rooms were finished and large new green gates had arrived.

At that point we needed to purchase beds, tables, chairs, sheets, everything it takes to run a house multiplied by fifty.

There were school supplies and uniforms to make—so much to do—so little time. September 6th was not far away.

Idris was planning a big opening day celebration and the entire village had been invited. Officials were coming from other regions and districts. There would be roasted lamb and lots of food and music. It would be a great celebration. Jesus' first miracle in the Bible was at Cana at a wedding feast, and I prayed He would show up at His house and do the same for us.

The van we rode in was uneasily quiet that hot August afternoon. Turkish music blared from the cassette player. Our driver was visibly

nervous as we prepared to leave the IHF office in Nazran, Ingushetia for our journey. He had good reason. He had agreed to smuggle our group of twelve into the Chechen republic so they could participate in the opening celebrations of Lamb's Home.

I had left Chechnya in June, and was now returning with a group which included my wife Dottie, our 10 year-old son Josiah, and our 8 year-old daughter, Elizabeth.

Not since 1997 had I attempted to travel into Chechnya with such a large group of Americans, and never before had I taken my family along. I was so sure the Lord had gathered us for this time, and being the fearless leader I pretended to be, I reassured the group the Lord was with us. I was full of faith—and fear. I turned up the music.

Leaving Nazran, Ingushetia we turned onto the infamous M29 road I had traveled many times before. Lying across my wife's lap, our daughter Elizabeth lay silent and pale. The day before a local doctor from a German humanitarian organization had diagnosed her with pneumonia and recommended that she not travel.

In the past I had visited many sick children in the refugee camps of Ingushetia and Chechnya. I had felt their fevered brows. We had brought them medicines. Now I was seeing my own daughter in a similar situation. Yet, by God's mercy, she had a clean bed to sleep in and she didn't have to breathe the foul air of a refugee camp.

After a long night of wrestling with our emotions, Dottie and I decided we couldn't leave her in Nazran. Dottie offered to stay with her at our office there, but I could not provide armed security for them. I could have never left them in Nazran.

Elizabeth insisted that she didn't want to stay either because she planned to tie balloon animals for the kids at the opening day ceremonies at Lamb's Home. She had made it this far, she said, and she would make it all the way.

Riding next to me in the front seat of the van was Hizer, one of Idris's brothers. Hizer was a pleasant man with a soft disposition. He had our documents and Russian rubles to slip into the passport which usually got us through the maze of Russian and Chechen military checkpoints. The standing joke was "It's easy to get into Chechnya—you just can't get out!

Hizer turned to me and said, "We are going to have to take a different road into Chechnya today. It is going to take us a couple of hours longer to drive."

I never like twist in a plan, especially with team members along. I like to be informed and know the plan in advance.

As I questioned Hizer's idea, he assured me that his intelligence was good and a friend had informed him before leaving Nazran to take this route as there was military activity on the regular route. The word "activity" in Chechnya is not good. I caught my wife's eye and could tell she was worried. Liz lay still.

Our van slowed as it approached the first OMON military checkpoint. I instructed the team not to talk, and if they were asked anything by the guards to let Helen handle any communication.

Stopping far short of the iron bar blocking the road so as not to give the soldiers a close look at us, our driver and Hizer collected our documents, got out and began walking towards the soldiers.

The soldiers looked at the numbers on the license plate of the vehicle, then began asking questions. "Documents! What are you doing here? Why are you driving an Ingush vehicle? Where are you going? Who is in the van? What are you carrying?"

The atmosphere among the team grew tense and we prayed for the Lord to protect and open the way.

I could see the captain turn to Hizer and put his hand out. With a sleight-of-hand Hizer transferred 200 rubles (the equivalent of about $5) to the captain., and a soldier lifted the iron bar and waved us through.

The driver ran back to the van and quickly drove us past the barricade before the soldier could change his mind and ask for more money. Was this an answer to prayer or bribery? I know that many Christians question this sort of thing, but I would never think of putting my family and co-workers at risk over the simple $5 "admission fee" the guard requested. After all, Jesus said to give unto Caesar what is Caesar's. At this checkpoint, the armed guard was Caesar.

As our van got a little closer to the post, peering into an opening in the makeshift concrete bunker so typical of the checkpoints, I saw the outline of a young soldier manning a heavy-caliber machine gun fix his sight on us. I prayed the young man was sober and not trigger happy. Vodka and guns don't mix, but you saw the combination everywhere, another reminder that we were crossing into Chechnya.

Driving in from the north side also meant that we would have to go directly through Grozny in order to get to the road that led south to Gikalo. This was very dangerous—there were many Russian troops and checkpoints in the city. There were also many snipers. Grozny was not a safe place. Through his informant, Hizer had arranged for a Chechen military security escort to accompany us through the city and then on to Gikalo.

By God's grace, the sharp eyes of our Chechen security guards, and by the speed and radical antics of our driver, we made it through Grozny. Before long we were on the south side of the city headed out of town and into the rural countryside near the village of Gikalo.

After a final checkpoint leaving Grozny proper, we were in the clear, relatively speaking. The tension eased a little as the gentle rolling hills began to mask and replace the locations where horrible events had destroyed the lives of so many over the last decade.

Just before the turnoff to the village was the cemetery. Rising above the normal burial mounds were the long steel poles with the Islamic crescent moon above them, marking the graves of the *Shahid*, or warriors—those who had died fighting the Russians for their homeland. In reverence, Hizer and our driver leaned forward as we passed the gravesites, bowing to honor the dead.

Turning off the main road we arrived at Gikalo. It had a pre-war population of about 3,000, but now, with the influx of families who had their homes and apartments destroyed in Grozny, the population had swelled to almost 5,000 people.

In a little village like this, news spreads fast - Americans had arrived in Gikalo. The van pulled up in front of a beautiful new brick wall and compound. I couldn't believe my eyes.

I had just been at the home here in June and the workers had just begun the brickwork for the building and now, only two months later, they had finished everything in time for the opening ceremony. It was truly a miracle. Idris came out to greet us beaming from ear to ear. " *Adircual!* Welcome! Welcome to Lamb's Home!" The workers and children came running out to greet us.

Also running to greet us was Malka, Maleka's sister, who was the head chef for Lamb's Home. With big hugs for Helen and Dottie, the lady workers greeted our ladies with smiles and beaming faces.

Several of the men workers, Saed, Saloudi, Doca, Boudi and Hamsat emerged from the building with warm handshakes for the men and my son.

Maleka soon arrived from their home in another part of the village. She immediately began to prepare a bed for my daughter and the other women pitched in to prepare hot tea and food for the team.

Chechen culture is steeped in hospitality and protection for their guests. Having entered the realm of Idris' family in Gikalo, we were now officially under the covering of their *tepe* or clan. Any provisions we needed or required were to be met by their family. All issues regarding our team's safety and protection fell under their responsibility and that of local Gikalo Chechen militia who were Special Forces men working for the Grozny region. They were good men, willing to risk their lives for us. I will never forget them.

Vacha, the captain, was dressed in blue camouflage and had a new Motorola radio tucked into his jacket. Every so often you could hear a voice coming across his radio, crackling in Chechen or Russian.

Adam was a skinny, mild-mannered newlywed fully outfitted in military fatigues. He was a devout Muslim.

Musa was short and stocky, dressed in blue jeans and leather jacket with a machine gun strapped over his shoulder.

Then there was Aslanbek, a massive man in his early thirties with a kind face and twinkle in his eye. Married, he and his wife

Tamara had three girls. He was also a Muslim, but not as devout as Adam.

They were all ready for action with Kalashnikov machine guns, ammo clips, impact grenades and flack jackets.

Malka called us into the kitchen and eating hall for hot *chai* (tea) and cookies. Dinner would come later, but for now the hot tea would serve to pick up our spirits. It didn't hurt either to have the chocolates that always go so well with Russian tea.

Idris officially welcomed the team to his village. He gave a brief talk on the upcoming plans for the next few days. He also stressed that as his guests he wanted us all to be safe and well. You could tell by his tone that he was worried about us.

While at the Lamb's Home compound, Idris and I insisted that absolutely no one go out of the compound gates. We instructed everyone that even if they had to visit the outside toilet (outhouse) at the back of the property, they needed to have a guard accompany them.

Although we were welcomed by the local authorities and village people, the fact remained that we were in Chechnya. Renegade mercenaries and mafia gangs had created a huge source of income by kidnapping aid workers, and had given Chechnya the dubious label of "Kidnapping Capitol of the World." We could not be naive to believe that our arrival in Gikalo had only been noticed by those who were our friends. There were intelligence agents everywhere.

Idris said, "Tomorrow we will officially open Lamb's Home for the orphan children of Chechnya. I have invited Akmed Khadirov, the president of Chechnya, as well as the mayor of Grozny, to attend. If they can't attend, they promised to send a delegation from their offices!"

I looked at Idris and smiled as if to say, "You're not serious are you?"

"I have," he said, "and they should come. You and your Christian friends came all the way from America to Chechnya, and are doing a great work for the Chechen people and our children. They can come across the republic to recognize your efforts. Shame on them if they don't come!"

I had heard before that Russian and Chechen politicians participated in such events because of the pomp and ceremony that put them in the limelight. They wanted the exposure, but I wanted to keep a low profile.

At that moment I saw Vacha grab his radio and gun and begin moving quickly towards our gate. Something serious was happening outside in the street. Vacha began to call out to Idris to come to the gate right away.

Barreling down the dirt street were two Russian OMON jeeps followed by a heavily armed APC carrier with a dozen Russian soldiers sitting on top, guns drawn and ready.

Some of the soldiers were wearing the black hoods pulled down over their faces to keep from being recognized. These guys were usually part of the elite Main Intelligence Directorate's (GRU) *Spetsnaz* brigades which were referred to by the Chechens as "Night Demons."

Banging along behind it was another military truck carrying more soldiers and a 75 mm anti-aircraft gun.

The trucks and jeeps rolled up to the gate and slid to a dusty stop. Stepping out of the lead jeep was a Russian Colonel and his driver. In a firm voice he asked, "Where is Idris? Is this where the children's home will open tomorrow? Have the Americans arrived yet?"

Idris hadn't been kidding. The Chechen president Akmed Khadirov wasn't coming but he sent several Chechen and Russian representatives in his place.

One was a Major in the FSB, Russia's Federal Service Bureau, or the successor of the KGB. All of these soldiers had been sent ahead to set up a security perimeter around the village to ensure the security of the representatives that would be arriving in the morning.

The soldiers dismounted from their vehicles and began fanning out around the home, building makeshift bunkers at all four corners of the property as well as positioning themselves at vantage points elsewhere.

In the matter of a few minutes, our "under the radar" arrival for the opening of Lamb's Home had gone from a quiet village ceremony with a few of the Muslim elders coming to hear why the Christians had come from America, to a official event guarded by enough fire power to start a small scale war.

I didn't like having all this extra attention, especially mixing the Russian soldiers with our Chechen militia guys. I also knew that this attention would put us on the radar of every bandit in the Caucuses. I could tell Vacha wasn't thrilled either; not because of ethnic issues, but because he knew the Russian soldiers drank vodka while on duty, and they could be trigger-happy in a drunken state.

The afternoon began to turn to dusk. The soldiers became restless. The night in Chechnya is when the demons come out to play. Most raids on the checkpoints happen at night. After dark no one travels on the roads. If they do, they never live to see the following day. Nightfall brings a fox-hole survival mentality. The cooks prepared a huge meal for the guards and plenty of black tea to keep them awake and alert.

Our team was tired and by now we were ready to eat and then have devotions together in the house where we would be sleeping. The house was a two-story building and we would be on the second floor in the back two rooms, away from the street. The house guards would sleep in the front and would post someone in the doorway. The entire front street was blocked off, and there were machine guns positioned at each corner of the building. Lamb's Home had been transformed into an armed fortress.

By the time dinner was served it was dark and the courtyard of the Lamb's Home compound took on a different look and feel. The electricity flickered in and out, eventually going off all together. Hizer went out back where we had a large Russian army generator wired into the building as a back-up for when the power went out. With a crank of the motor, the generator fired up and we had light again, although much dimmer than before. The events of the following day were shaping up to be big, and we needed our rest.

Our daughter Liz was already bunked down for the night in the back bedroom. Seeing her sick, Maleka had launched a major campaign of home remedies to try and get her well. Malka and the women in the kitchen had prepared corn silk soup with chicken broth for her to eat. Idris had rubbed her feet down with pure spirits of alcohol and then wrapped her feet to draw out any fever from her body. More prayers were being offered over her than could be imagined. Even though she didn't like being sick, I think she liked all the attention.

Goodnights were said to Malka and the ladies in the kitchen. Well wishes for safety were given to the guards—no sweet dreams for them.

Vacha and Bekhan came up to our room to wish us good sleep and to reassure us that he and the guards were in control of everything, and that we need not worry.

As he closed the door and stepped back out into the night I could see the glow of his cigarette. He was smoking it fast and hard indication of his nervousness. The pressure was on.

The street was dark and artillery gunfire could be heard in the distance towards Grozny and the mountains to the south of us. This was a common occurrence at night. Tonight it seemed really close. Too close.

Idris and Maleka left to go back to their home and children just a couple of blocks away from Lamb's Home. Hizer would stay throughout the night in case anything was needed. Any other time, the wire springs on our bunk beds would have bugged me. That night it was a welcomed feeling to stretch out and close my eyes.

It felt as if I had just closed my eyes when I was suddenly jolted by the percussion and thunderous sound of an explosion that rattled the house and shook us from our sleep. My trusty REI wristwatch read 2:13 a.m.

At first I thought it might have been a gas line that had burst. However, as I leaped to my feet and ran toward the window I could hear Vacha and several of the other guards shouting at someone down the street.

Suddenly all hell broke loose. Machine gun fire erupted from every position, lighting up the street and surrounding area. Fear gripped my heart. Was this some paramilitary Chechen rebel group staging an attempt to take the Americans hostage for political gain with Russia? Was it local Chechen fighters who had heard that there was a company of Russian boys down at the Lamb's Home and they just wanted to make their night interesting? In that confused moment, no one knew.

The dire thoughts faded as it became clear that all of the fire was outgoing. It did not, however, make the situation any less unnerving or frightening.

At the first sound of gunfire, Dottie had pulled Elizabeth from the top bunk and thrown herself over her, and they were both under the bed.

The other ladies had crawled across the floor up against the wall furthest from the window. I could hear serious praying going on from all corners of the upstairs sleeping quarters.

I even thought I heard some praying in unknown languages. It didn't really matter to me at the time, just as long as they were praying. This was no time to dispute doctrine. Everyone was praying except for my son Josiah—not that he wouldn't have prayed, but he was still sound asleep. I guess he was more like Jesus than the rest of us, sleeping through the storm.

I looked out the window and began calling out to Bekhan to give me some kind of report about what was going on.

"No worry David, we repel the bandits, you can go back to sleep," Bekhan called out.

Bandits, what bandits? Sleep? Are you kidding me—after all that you expect us to just relax and go back to sleep? Later I would learn that Vacha had shot a grenade at what he thought was someone sneaking up the street towards the home. We would never know the entire story, and perhaps it was better that way.

The night calmed and we lay back down. Staring at the ceiling we prayed for the Lord to quiet everyone's nerves and to give us peace in our hearts. We knew that God had brought us to Chechnya and His angels were around about those who feared Him. We also prayed for the Lord to give us opportunities to share the gospel with the soldiers that were keeping watch over us. As I said, "Amen," we could hear the distinct thunder of Russian tank fire echoing off the nearby hillside. We prayed for the morning light.

Construction Begins at Lambs Home -2001

Chechen brick masons

"The Fish"

Chapter 7

Dancing Days

The laughter of children mixed with the crowing of a rooster served as our alarm clock.

Today we would celebrate the opening of Lamb's Home.

The Russian soldiers were already patrolling the street outside, securing the surrounding area for the FSB officers that would be coming later.

Malka was busy in the kitchen preparing breakfast for the guards and organizing the meal for later that afternoon. Kuri, another one of Idris' brothers, backed his truck into the courtyard. Something inside was moving.

All the children were running around excited about what Kuri had in the back of the truck. " *Baran! Baran!*" they shouted.

Lifting up the cover on the truck we saw two beautiful sheep with curled horns, one with black and white markings, the other white all over. In Chechnya, as well as many other Islamic cultures, offering a ram is the highest form of hospitality you can show to your guest.

In honor of this special day, these two rams would be prepared for the afternoon meal. One would be roasted on long skewers, better known as *shoshleek*. The other would be sectioned and then boiled in a large black caldron.

By preparing the meal in this way, the elders from the local mosque could come and enjoy the meal as well. Some of the elders were over one hundred years old and at that age the gums need all the help they could get!

The ritual associated with preparing this type of meal is fascinating. Saloudi, one of our workers, had been chosen to do the honors. After laying the ram on its side, he took a sharp knife and placed his hand upon the head of the ram. He then recited a verse from the *Koran* and blessed the gift of life that would be lost in order for it to bring life to those who ate it.

Saloudi then gave thanks on behalf of the one who offered it, and with a swift stroke he cut the throat of the ram. The bright red blood spurted onto the ground as the ram gave its last drop of life. Like the Old and New Testaments declare, the blood is shed so that we might live.

The next step was to hang the ram up much like you would a deer, skinning and removing all of the internal organs. Afterwards the meat was chopped into smaller pieces and left in a bucket mixed with onions, garlic, vinegar and a touch of basil or parsley. There it would marinate for a few hours before being skewered onto long metal spears called *champuras* and cooked over an open fire. Whether you liked lamb or not, this was a meal you didn't want to miss.

While the men prepared to cook the meat out back, Malka and the other ladies were hard at work in the kitchen preparing for the lunch and dinner that would be served today.

Other Lamb's Home ladies were working on a small program that the Lamb's Home children would perform after lunch. Chechens are known for their love of food and lively dancing. We would have both this day. With the FSB big brass coming from the city of Tolstoy Yurt, and with Americans in town, no effort would be spared. This was to be a day of feasting that would be long remembered.

The warm August sun was nearing its zenith when, as promised, the Chechen FSB officials arrived for the opening day ceremony. In typical Caucasus fanfare, their Toyota 4Runners and APCs raced down the little dirt road in front of Lamb's Home creating a dust cloud enveloping the Russian soldiers riding on top.

The guards already at the home tensed as they readied for their commanders to arrive. The additional soldiers, bare-armed and wearing pirate bandanas, were packing heavy weapons. Skidding to a stop just outside our gate, you would have thought that they were preparing for the shootout at the OK Corral.

Hizer, Idris and I went out to meet the officials. The doors to his 4Runner swung open and several men stepped out. One was a short portly man, slightly balding and in his early fifties I guessed. He was well dressed in a nice Italian suit and was sporting a pistol in a Bianca harness on his left shoulder. I couldn't tell if he was Chechen or not, but from the way the rest of the men treated him, I could tell he was the boss.

The next man was tall, well built, and was wearing a Russian commando uniform with two stars on each shoulder. He was from Moscow, and in charge of the Russian *Speznat* in the Grozny region.

The third was a dark-skinned Chechen man from the local administration in the village. He also was packing a sidearm. Each greeted us in a friendly manner.

"Welcome to Lamb's Home, the best rehabilitation center for children in the entire Chechen Republic," Idris said.

By now, the place was alive with excitement as the entourage of security guards and officials moved from the street into the courtyard of the compound.

I introduced my wife Dottie and our children to them, as well as the rest of our American team.

My son Josiah and some of the Chechen boys from Lamb's Home were kicking a soccer ball around in the courtyard. Kids were running around with balloons shaped like animals, compliments of my daughter Elizabeth. By God's grace, she had recovered from her sickness almost overnight. Even though she was still weak, God had granted her wish to be able to participate in all the events of the day. Even the Chechen women were amazed to see how quickly she had recovered. They had witnessed our team praying over her the day before. Now, some asked if our prayers were the cause of her remarkable improvement.

Out in the back of the property, the men were busy tending to the boiling pots of lamb and potatoes that were being prepared for the elders that would soon come from the local mosque.

Lechi, another one of our workers, was sweating in the August sun as he prepared the skewers of *shoshleek* over the open pit of fiery coals. Some of the Russian soldiers had relaxed their vigil of protection and were mingling with our team, asking questions about America and about what kind of cars we drove.

The setting was surreal. Americans, Russians, Chechens—Christians, Orthodox, Muslims— in the war zone of Chechnya along with laughing children and their animal shaped balloons and soccer balls. Without God's divine presence, the thought of this kind of event would be insane. My mind went back to the time when we had planned this day and I had prayed that just as Jesus had come to the wedding at Cana, that He would also join us that day. He had heard that prayer. He was there. The miracle was happening.

Inside, Malka and the other women had prepared an incredible meal. The table was graced with fresh onions, cucumbers, peppers, tomatoes, garlic and warm *lavash*, (flat bread). It was a sight to behold. Also, in typical Caucasus tradition, there was vodka and cognac for toasting the coming of the guests from America and the opening of the home. Now, with all preparations complete and the guests assembled, we were invited to sit down at the table. I stood and asked God to bless our work and the food. With a hearty "Amen" from the Americans, Lechi brought in the first sizzling skewers of *shoshleek* and sat them down on the platter of onions and garlic in the middle of the table. It was Cana all over again!

In this eastern culture, the guests sit at the head of the table, then from left to right in importance. Idris placed me at the head with Dottie next to me. Then the FSB boss, the Russian colonel, the local Chechen administrator and so on. It was a stressful situation but God intended it to be this way as I was about to find out.

Aslan, my Chechen translator was seated to my right. As was their custom, the host was to make an opening toast honoring the guests for coming to their home. Idris took the lead by pouring a small glass for me and the FSB officer.

I was pleased the officials from Grozny had come. I wanted them to know our intentions and hear the gospel of Jesus Christ, maybe for the first time—and possibly last time— in their lives. I knew that God had foreordained this day and this feast for His divine purposes. I wanted to enter into their world as Jesus would, as their friend. Yes, the friend of wine bibbers, sitting with them, in the house of Matthew and Zacheus, where sinners and tax collectors hung out. They needed the doctor. But I also didn't want to blow my testimony either, so I participated in a way that would honor the Lord. I would have to be very careful seeing the wine of Cana was a wee bit stronger today.

The table was like a beehive. Lechi continued to bring in sizzling hot skewers of lamb from out back. Mixed in with fresh onions and lots of garlic, the aroma from the table was thick with tradition.

Soon another toast was proposed, this time for the success and blessing on our work, both with the children at the home and in the republic itself.

At this point the FSB officer began to ask me some very pointed questions about our intentions of working in the republic, and about who was sponsoring our organization. His stern tone and unflinching eye contact told me he was probing for intelligence that would reveal any false representation of who we really were.

He went into this long discourse on how the FSB was keeping a very watchful eye on any organizations posing as humanitarian aid workers trying to get into Chechnya for espionage reasons. Several high profile organizations such as Amnesty International and Human Rights Watch were publishing first-hand reports from refugees about systematic torture and human rights violations being committed by Russia's forces. Putin's refusal to allow journalists, Russian or foreign, to cover the war only added to the suspicions of cover-up and was severely damaging their justification of the war itself. It was also rumored that Russia was testing new military equipment and wanted it surrounded with total secrecy. In the past, several groups working under humanitarian cover had been revealed to be supplying intelligence to Europe, the U.S.A. and Britain.

"We are thankful that you and your Christian friends from America have such a love for the Chechen and Russian people in this republic. You are welcome to come, and if you notify us when you will come, we will do everything in our power to help you remain safe and protected. We need people like you to come and help us restore hope in our hearts.

He then spoke in a more threatening manner. " But if we find out that you are working for the CIA or the NSA from America or MI-6," he said, "I guarantee you that we will find you and put you in prison for spying on Russia!" With these words he downed another shot of vodka.

This was the opening I had been waiting for. I spoke to him in tone that would convey the depths of my convictions.

I said, "I know you are suspicious and have a hard time trusting anyone or anything. The Soviet system created this in you. But as God is my witness, I can assure you that our group is here for one thing, to tell you and anyone else who listens that there is a God who loves you and He gave His son to die for you. You can believe that and rest your life upon it. Jesus Christ is the only hope for you and Chechen people. I have one mission, and that is to show you and the Chechen people the love of God through my actions and His love. And, as for who I work for, I am employed by the kingdom of heaven, not America. My nationality may be American, but my allegiance is to the kingdom over which Jesus reigns. We are sponsored by Christians in America who give of their personal finances and time to help us share the gospel of Jesus Christ. In fact, there are small children who give of their money to help the children in Chechnya. You need not worry about me or our any of our team gathering intelligence for the CIA or MI-6."

He sat silent, staring into his shot glass. Looking up he said, "I believe you are telling me the truth. I will consider what you have told me today."

For a brief moment it seemed his heart had been touched by the Holy Spirit. The mood at the table had settled into a quiet reverence during our conversation. It was clear that Holy Spirit had taken my words far beyond just the ears of this FSB man.

I know that all sitting around the table that day heard the gospel of Jesus Christ loud and clear. Hopefully it found a place in all their hearts. The seeds of the gospel had been planted and I prayed that the Lord would do His work and cause those seeds to grow and come to fruition.

We sat around the table until everyone had eaten their fill. It was then time to clear the table and open up the floor for the program from the children and from our group. Many other visitors from the village had joined us. There must have been at least fifty adults now lining the walls of the hall listening to the music.

The kids sang a special song about the war in Chechnya and how they wished it had never happened. The innocence of their voices somehow made the words so much more pathetic and tragic.

I glanced over once and saw several of the soldiers wipe tears from their eyes. It was a moving moment. Following their song, our group shared a couple Christian worship songs. Since there were so many new people that had come in, I felt led to share a gospel message once again. There wasn't an altar call given, but God's presence was touching hearts. His word wouldn't return void.

Just then the dark-skinned man from the local administration jumped to his feet and began clapping his hands. That was the signal for some Chechen dancing. Soon accordion music filled the room with a spirited rhythm and people began to move in the graceful patterns of the Chechen dance. Usually between the male and the female partners, this dance is steeped in ancient Caucasus tradition and symbolizes two eagles in flight.

The official was so into his dancing, and perhaps because he had toasted one too many toasts, he whipped out his pistol and shot two rounds through the ceiling! I know that shooting into the air is a Middle Eastern and Caucasus tradition at weddings and celebrations, but inside a room with children around? It was insane.

Two of the guards came running in response to the shots. They were quickly briefed on the incident and after the initial shock, calm was restored. If it hadn't been so serious, it would've been funny. I had brought my wife and kids to Chechnya along with a team to dedicate a children's home and one of us could have died from a bullet fired by a dancing Chechen. Angels were watching over us.

Having survived the mild interrogation from the FSB officer and the bullets on the dance floor, I was exhausted. I stepped outside into the courtyard to get some fresh air.

Within a couple of hours, Kiem and the elders from the mosque would come over. That would create another intense time of spiritual opportunity, but I wasn't sure I was ready. Suddenly I felt drained. The events of the last few days were catching up with me. The travel, the responsibility of a team and my family in Chechnya, the sheer scope of the ministry we were involved in—it was overwhelming.

The afternoon began to fade into early evening. The food consumed, the dancing over, the guests began to leave one by one. The FSB officers bid us farewell and began to organize their security details to leave. They didn't want to travel through Grozny at night, so they needed to leave as soon as possible. With the same military fanfare that they had arrived, their entourage of soldiers and security guards massed in front of Lamb's Home. Shaking hands and bidding them a safe journey back, we stood in the road and waved goodbye. In a cloud of dust and black diesel smoke from their APC, their convoy sped away like a posse into the sunset, the silhouettes of soldiers and guns disappearing as they went.

Walking back through the big green gates into the courtyard, Idris lit a cigarette. We were both emotionally spent. Hosting these officials was important for the official status of the home, but Idris and I both knew that having these FSB people breathing down our necks was like dancing with the devil. The men that had come to the lunch that day could be the same men that could work behind the scenes to make our work very difficult. We both breathed a sigh of relief that they were gone, at least for now. My FSB file probably grew by a dozen pages that day.

The Muslim elders gave no warning of their arrival like the FSB men did. They didn't come with military fanfare. Walking in silence, they came one by one. Chechen men, ranging in age from 40 to 107.

They all wore beards and *papaka*, the traditional Chechen hat made of lamb's wool.

The men entered quietly and reverently, each greeting us in a calm voice. They then greeted each other. There were about twenty in all.

The dining hall once again became a feasting place. This time, however, the eating arrangements were much different. Rather than a table, the men all sat on the floor in a circle that started with the eldest to the youngest.

None of our team would eat with them as this meal was strictly a ceremony that only the elders were allowed to participate in. It was their way of saying to us that they blessed our work and presence in their village.

As they took their rightful seats, Malka and the kitchen ladies began to bring out the boiled lamb that had been cooked earlier in the day. Hot bread and plates of the traditional Chechen dish called *gigi galish*, small flour dumplings dipped in strong garlic bouillon and eaten with dried beef, were also part of the evening's fare. Only carbonated water and cola were served to drink. No vodka toast for Muslims, at least not in public.

Sitting at the head of the circle was an elder who looked to be the youngest. His eyes dark and somber, and his hair and beard dark black. He seemed to be the spiritual leader of the group since once the eating was over he began to direct the group into what the Chechens call the *Zikr*. This traditional ritual is performed only by the Sufi branch of Chechen Muslims at their weddings, funerals, or before going into battle or other special events.

The only way I can describe it—imagine twenty men chanting and dancing, trancelike, while moving in unison, in a circular motion, like a wheel spinning in place. How they do this without stepping on each other is a mystery. I have heard that the Swirling Dervishes in Turkey derived their trance-like dance from the Chechen tradition of *Zikr*.

After a half an hour or so, they stopped their chanting and dancing. I asked one of their men the significance of this dance.

He said, "When we do the *Zikr*, we feel we are closer to God and that we are earning His approval. It shows our piety. The circular motion shows completeness. By dancing, we feel we are trampling our sins under our feet."

His words saddened my heart as I realized here were men trying to earn God's favor and grace though a ritual. I asked if I could share a word with them before they left. Kiem graciously obliged.

Straight to the point, I said, "Elders of Gikalo, you are Muslims. My friends and I are followers of Jesus, or Isa as you know him in the *Koran*. You call me a 'Child of the Book.' You know Isa as a good man, even a prophet from God. But He is more than a good man and a prophet. He is God. You can know Him and have fellowship with Him. There is a way to have God's approval without works or the *Zikr*. It is through believing in Isa, Jesus Christ."

The room was quiet. I made eye contact with the elder with the dark eyes and dark beard. He stared back. I wasn't sure what he was thinking but I don't think it was positive. It didn't matter. I could sense many of the others had taken to heart what I said and even Kiem, the head teacher of the mosque, looked as if God's Spirit had moved him.

That said, Kiem and the elders thanked us for the invitation to come to our celebration and for the meal. I thanked them for honoring us with their presence. Then, just as they had come, they left. Quietly we walked them out to the gate and bid them farewell.

Night was approaching quickly. Lechi and a couple of the Chechen militia guards were hanging around out back by the fire that still burned from earlier in the day. Malka and most of the ladies had retreated into the kitchen for a cup of tea and some much needed rest. The nannies were putting the kids to bed. Idris and Maleka had gone home. For once, in what seemed like days, it seemed strangely calm and quiet. Our team had retreated back upstairs in the house to finish out the day with devotions. We were spent, emotionally, physically and spiritually. Our official Lamb's Home opening celebration was over, but our dancing days were just beginning.

LeCompte Family – Opening Day Lambs Home

Chapter 8

The Children of Lamb's Home

We loved children, but we had no experience in managing a children's home. I knew the Lord wanted this place to come into being since my first visit to the refugee sanatorium in Nalchik, where I had met Nasan, the eight-year-old with ebony eyes, and the other suffering Chechen children there. I felt humbled that the Lord had brought His plan to fruition through me and the people who supported IHF.

There had been a second deadly war since that first visit, and our ministry had experienced hardship and adversity over the intervening years. I had been in personal peril on scores of occasions, and team members under my care had also been at risk. But we were seeing the ultimate fruit of our labors now, as we gathered orphans and other at-risk Chechen children into the fold at Lamb's Home.

We knew that Jesus said to love and care for orphans and there were a lot of them in Chechnya. It was clear to us that this was one of the ways that we could show God's love to the people of this region. That is why Lamb's Home existed.

Every child who came to Lamb's Home had a story, some more heartbreaking than others. Some left a mark on my heart forever.

Linda and Emani were sisters, ten and nine years old, we think. Their birth certificates were destroyed and their mother had died of tuberculosis.

When Hizir found them in Gudermes, a city near Grozny, they were living with an abusive uncle. Linda was mildly retarded and Emani was violent and uncontrollable.

Their haircuts were boyish and unkempt. Linda was the spitting image of a little Jerry Lewis, and Linda was always "Jerry" to me.

On their first day at Lamb's Home, Linda sat in the corner staring at the floor. Emani bit four boys and one nanny, drawing blood from one.

Emani released herself in a motherly embrace from Dottie, and she could tell all Emani needed was a little affection. We had no degrees in psychology or therapy, so that is all we had to give.

In two years, God's love transformed the girls into sweet young ladies. Linda and Emani were a miracle.

Linda became more studious, and though she struggled mentally, her grades in school improved and she was more social with the other kids.

Emanis' spirit changed from night to day. She bloomed into a beautiful young girl and became responsible to help care for the other children that came to us. She excelled in the Chechen cultural arts of dancing and singing.

People would bring children to Lamb's Home all the time. It was up to Hizir to discern what children to take and which to refuse. We couldn't care for the entire Chechen republic, although we tried sometimes. It was one of his toughest jobs.

One day an old Chechen man came to the gate and asked to see the Hizir. He wasn't alone. In tow was a skinny little Russian boy the old man had caught stealing potatoes in the central market of Grozny.

"I don't know his name, and he won't tell me what it is," the man said. "He is a good kid but needs help. I am too old and have no place to raise him. You must take him and train him to be a man."

Before Hizir could say no, the old man turned and walked out the gate, never to be seen again.

With sad eyes and a face full of mischief, the boy sat staring at Hizir. The standoff lasted a few minutes until the boy blinked. Hizir smiled and said, "Welcome, from now on you will be called Ramzan. You can stay here at Lamb's Home and will be part of our family"

The boy sat quietly, thinking. After a few minutes of silence the boy responded, "I am Ramzan. I will live here with you. You will be my family now."

Ramzan was a good kid, but he had his problems. He had survived on the streets for so long that stealing was second nature to him. Coming to Lamb's Home just gave him a new venue to practice his trade. He learned quickly the system, and what he could and couldn't get away with at the home.

Cooking utensils became his favorite item to lift. The kitchen workers would find items missing, only to have them turn up in the local bazaar for sale.

Hizir finally figured out the scheme. Ramzan was stealing utensils from our kitchen, then taking them to school where his friends, other 11 year-old children, would take them into the market. They all were in on the fun. Once caught, Hizir dealt sternly and broke the cycle of theft.

Over a long time and with much patient love, Ramzan began to see that he didn't have to steal to live. He was also becoming more interested in listening to the Bible stories we told him, and he looked forward to IHF summer camps. Sometimes during our visits to Lamb's Home, we would find Ramzan by himself reading his Bible and teaching himself English.

His grades in school improved and the teachers were amazed at the progress he made. He began to assume more responsibility by helping in the kitchen and keeping the other younger boys in line. Ramzan had truly become part of the family.

Mikheil, Heda and Monsur are two brothers and a sister. They have the most heart-wrenching story of all the kids that came to Lamb's Home.

They were brought to us riding in a sidecar of a policeman's motorcycle. He rescued them from a remote mountain village that had seen days and days of fighting and artillery attacks. Their mother had been wounded by a piece of shrapnel and was paralyzed from the neck down. The father had run away. Later he was found dead in the city of Argun, run over by a truck while on a drunken binge.

All of the neighbors had fled the fighting in the village, so no one was left to take care of the mom except the children. As winter set in, the oldest boy Mikhiel, 10 years old, dragged his invalid mother into a vacant mud thatched house to care for her and his younger siblings, Heda, 9 and Monsur, 7. The house was more like a dirt hut and was not fit for animals to live in.

Their mom weakened and she became bedridden and was eaten up with bed sores. Her sheets were soiled and filthy. She was cold and helpless.

No one knew why the children didn't tell anyone about their mom. Maybe they were ashamed of their plight and so they had decided to take care of her themselves. By the time they were found, they were beyond dirty, barefooted, malnourished and had very little clothing on. They were also in a state of shock from the trauma of watching their mother waste away, not knowing what to do or who to ask for help.

That day at the home they found the help they needed. We took them in clothed and fed them and gave them and a warm and secure environment to heal and grow.

Esama embodied all that we were trying to accomplish at Lamb's Home. She was an orphan with only a distant aunt as a relative. When she came to Lamb's Home she was 11 years old. With beautiful chestnut brown hair, a soft smile and sweet spirit, she captured everyone's heart right away. I met her for the first time during our Christmas program in January 2003. She had just been brought to the home and was still trying to fit in with the other children.

Whenever Lamb's Home kids had a special event, the cultural dancing of Chechnya was always something that happened naturally. From an early age Chechen children participate in this art and it is a beautiful thing to behold. As a young girl Esama was particularly graceful at this dance and all the boys wanted to dance with her.

Esama seemed to understand and embrace the gospel message. She was about fourteen and I remember the day when this became evident to me. We were teaching Bible stories at our IHF summer camp at Mt. Elbrus, Balkaria. To illustrate the lessons, we would take the kids out by the river or up into the mountains. This particular day we were by the river. The lesson was about Zacchaeus and Jesus coming home with him for dinner. My friend Mike, a brother from Calvary Community Church in Arizona, who had been with us on several trips, was teaching.

Mike asked what it meant when Jesus wanted to come home with Zacchaeus.

Esama blurted out, "That means that Jesus wants to come into your heart not just your head."

For a moment all of us looked at each other in disbelief. I knew that she had understood. I believe that day God did something in Esama. We did not lead her in the sinner's prayer, nor did we take her name and address for follow up or give her a new believer packet. We did create an environment so she could be cared for, and by God's grace, I believe she will never forget her experience.

Two years later, at the same camp, at the same place by the river, Esama came to me after a similar Bible story. Rumors were flying that she would be leaving Lamb's Home after the summer camp. Her distant aunt was reclaiming her and there was no way the staff at Lamb's Home could stop it.

Everyone, including myself, was upset about this turn of events. Sitting on a large boulder by the river, Esama handed me a small bouquet of Caucasus Mountain wildflowers. She had picked them herself and giving them to me she started to softly cry.

Gathering herself she said, "David, thank you for bringing your friends from America to help me. You have taught me that Jesus loves me and that He will watch over me, no matter where I go. Even in Chechnya. I will never forget you and your family. Please don't forget me." And with those words she walked away to rejoin the other girls.

I often think about Esama. After her aunt came and took her away in the fall of 2005, our staff didn't hear much from her. One of the workers heard she had been given away in marriage. We don't know. What I do know is that she knows that God loves her and that she understood the gospel from her time at Lamb's Home. I pray she never forgets the meaning of the story of Jesus going home with Zacchaeus.

Like a pack of stray dogs the five little boys crawled out of Hizir's car. The oldest, Akmad, was 10, the youngest, Said, was 2. There were three in the middle, Sultan, 8, Amir, slightly retarded, was 7, and Dinor was 5.

They were a wild bunch; they were found living in a rat infested basement without water, bare footed and had rags for clothes. Their hair was matted with lice and two of them had strange skin rashes. Filthy from head to toe, it took three baths to clean them.

A staff member put shoes on them. Having never worn shoes, the two younger ones immediately took them off. When shown the toilets, they drank the water out of them.

They had never been to school and had a difficult time socializing with the other children at the home. They only knew survival. This is how they came to Lamb's Home.

Through the grace and love of God, these boys slowly began to adapt and adjust to life at the home. Soon they were getting better grades in school and socializing with others in positive ways. As they continued to grow and mature, the eldest boy, Akmed, began to care for his younger siblings.

Following the example of the older men in the village, he grew into a young man because there were caring people both in America and in Chechnya who were willing to give him a chance.

Of course, there were many more who passed though the green gates of Lamb's Home. Some were with us for a short time, others for years. It was always our prayer that the Lord would send us children who had open hearts for the Gospel, and we did everything we could to show the love of Christ to them. Virtually all of them came to us in a hopeless state, but they left knowing that there was hope in Jesus Christ.

David & Lambs Home kids

Children and staff of Lambs Home

5 brothers

Heda, Michal and Monsur with IHF worker

Chapter 9

The Elder

A year passed. The opening day festivities this September would be very low key. There were no big celebrations, no FSB people, no American group. It was just me, the children, Idris and Maleka and the local people of Gikalo.

Taking advantage of this quietness, I had asked Hizir if he would arrange for the local Muslim elders to come to the home for a meal. I wanted to give them the opportunity to address any questions they had regarding Lamb's Home and our work among the orphans.

There must be a very specific reason for the elders to gather, as this is the custom in Chechnya. It must be a holy prayer day, a wedding, or the funeral of a family member. To gather just for the sake of gathering is not common and I was pleasantly surprised when Hizir told me that they had agreed to come. They would arrive after their Friday prayers.

Kiem, the head mullah, wanted to talk to me in front of the entire council. This was a first. Although they regarded me as a "Child of the Book," they very rarely permitted a non-Muslim to sit in on their gatherings or address the elders. I had long waited for the opportunity to address these men one-on-one. So sure was I that the Lord would answer my prayer to speak to them in this way that I had brought a Bible in the Chechen language for each of them.

After their prayers at the mosque, they began to arrive at Lamb's Home like Snow White's dwarves, from the oldest to the youngest.

The oldest man in the village was 107 years old. Born in 1895, he had survived some of the most turbulent times in history. He had seen the rise and fall of the Soviet Union, as well as both World Wars. He had lived through Stalin's purge and the Chechen deportation of 1945. Yet, he was just a few months older than several other elders who were also over the century mark. In fact, there are many centenarians in the Chechen republic, particularly in our village. Slowly, the others came and by the time they had finished gathering there was a group of 20 or more.

To show our respect, we had purchased a lamb from the market that morning, slaughtered it, and boiled the meat in huge pots.

Traditionally, the meat was served with bread, candies and other fruits. Gathering inside Lamb's Home, we had removed the eating tables, and a huge oriental rug had been laid out.

As the old men came in they took their seats sitting cross-legged on the rug according to age. Some sported traditional close beards but most were clean shaven. All had their prayer caps on. Most Chechen's aren't fundamentalist, but are of the Sufi branch, a group which takes a mystical approach to their observance of the Islamic traditions.

As they began to eat the oldest of the group invited me to join them. This was viewed by many as an honor, as not many of the locals are invited to join this meal. I accepted and took my place in the middle of the floor as a guest. My Chechen interpreter, an IHF office worker, Ruslan, joined me.

Ruslan had never participated in a meal with the elders before and he was extremely nervous. "Ruslan, don't be afraid," I said. "Translate every word I say, exactly like I say it! If you don't, I'll fire you!"

Although I was kidding, I wanted him to know that I was serious. This was a critical opportunity to share the message of Christ with these men. I didn't want anything left out.

Sitting cross-legged in the middle of the room, I was in the hot seat. The workers were bringing food into the room and placing it in front of the elders. I could feel their eyes as they looked me over, waiting to see what my reaction would be to their stares. A tradition in the eastern world is to never look away from eye contact. Doing so means you are not an honest person.

One of the old men across from me asked me to open a bottle of mineral water for him. Most bottled water in Russia is naturally carbonated and must be opened slowly so you don't spray the water everywhere. You would think, as long as I have worked in Russia, I would have been careful opening the bottle. However, without thinking, I reached over and quickly twisted off the cap. The bottle erupted, sending a shower of mineral water in every direction. The spray went all over the old man, me, and several others who were unfortunate enough to be in its path!

Startled, we both sat there staring at each other, mineral water dripping from our faces. It felt like an eternity, but he then burst out into laughter, and the rest of the council followed. It was the ice breaker we needed. From then on, the atmosphere was more relaxed—and I was more careful opening the next bottle of water.

After the meal, the elders began to talk about the work we were doing at Lamb's Home. They began by saying how much they appreciated our group coming to help the Chechen orphans and that they were supportive of our efforts.

Then came the questions I had hoped would be asked. The head elder asked, "Why do you want to be here? You are Christian, we are Muslims. Do you want to convert our children to your religion?"

I smiled at Ruslan.

He glared back as if to say, "You sure you want to go there?"

In response I said, "I first came to Chechnya in 1997. You did not know me, nor did I know you, yet I came. Not because I felt sorry for you or your people, but because I am a Christian and a follower of Jesus, You know him as Isa. He also commands me to love my neighbor as myself, to have compassion on those who are in need, to care for orphans and widows. This is pure religion before God. Your *Koran* tells you as much."

I knew I was headed into serious territory with these men, but I felt empowered by the Holy Spirit to continue. "I am not religious," I said, "nor am I hired by a church or religious organization to come here. In fact, no one could pay me enough money to risk coming here. I come here because Jesus died for me and you. He also came and died for the Chechen people, to give you a hope and the guarantee of eternal life."

I then thought to point out something I hoped would be obvious to them, a clear distinction between those who followed Christ, and those who were just religious zealots.

I said, "You know religious people don't come here. In fact, I haven't met any of the religious people who claim to be your brothers, the Muslims from Saudi Arabia and the other Islamic countries. They don't come here unless they are recruiting your young men to fight for their causes somewhere else, like Afghanistan, Iraq or Pakistan. They are the ones who are tearing your people apart. That is why I say that I am not here as a religious person."

I spoke to my own fears and as well as my faith in Christ when I said, "I am here to share my life as a Christian with you, the children, and the people of Chechnya. I will eat with you, cry with you, suffer injustice with you. If need be, I will die here. By doing this, if you see in me something that you believe is real and want to believe too, then you could say that you are converted. That is between you and God."

Muslims have a great fear that their people will convert to the Christian faith if given the opportunity, and that is why there are prohibitions against Christians sharing their faith in so many Muslim countries. I felt I needed to address that question, which I knew was in the minds of these elders.

I said, "If some of the workers or the children here in the home see something they can believe in that gives them hope and peace with God, I guess that would also qualify as conversion. If through the Bibles or the Christian videos that we have given them they choose to believe in Jesus, then they will make that decision on their own.

If through our good works you see that there is a real God, who gave His son Jesus, as the real sacrifice for all of our sins, then I will have achieved my goal. But to say that I am here to force anyone to believe like I do, I am not. That is religion, not life. I am only going to give away the life that Jesus Christ has given me. You are welcomed to receive it or refuse it. That is all".

As Ruslan finished the translation, sweat was beading on his forehead. I think he was having visions of Allah's sword descending upon his neck!

The room was silent. I knew that the words I had just spoken were of God and not of me. They had driven straight into the hearts of everyone there. The elders had seen our IHF people. My wife and kids had visited Lamb's Home along with others. They had witnessed the changes in the lives of the orphans and other at-risk children that had come to the home. They knew that we were not just fair weather friends, and that our mission was good and upright. They knew we were not ashamed to testify to our faith. Our works confirmed our faith.

All of the men sat silent, waiting for the eldest to speak, as was his right. The 107 year-old man reached feebly for his walking cane and struggled to his feet.

Leaning on his cane, he spoke simple words. He said, "I am Chechen, I am Muslim. I have lived a long time. I have lived through famines, wars, and the deportation of 1945. Now I am old and my days are short. I have seen and heard many people in my time claiming to be Christians. Today is the first day I have ever met one face to face. You may continue to help our people, young man, we need this message you bring."

After he spoke those words he shuffled out of the room.

Following his lead, the others voiced their approval. As they stood, each waited for the other, leaving by age, the eldest to the youngest. Filing out into the courtyard of Lamb's Home, they assembled to participate in the *Zikr*, where they chanted and danced in a moving circle, spinning like a wheel in unison.

Once the *Zikr* was finished, I thanked the elders of Gikalo for coming. As they turned to leave I embraced each one with a copy of the Bible in their language.

The 107 year-old elder came over to me and with hands trembling and a twinkle in his eye. He grabbed my hand and said, "Not only have I met a Christian for the first time today, but this is the first Bible I have ever seen in my own language. Thank you so much."

More than just answering questions about our work at Lamb's Home that day, the old Chechen elders had heard the gospel message. For one, it had taken 107 years to hear it for the very first time!

David and 107 year old Chechen elder

Chapter 10

Maleka's Child

The needs of the orphan children at Lamb's Home were foremost in our minds, but that did not stop IHF from demonstrating the love of Christ to others in Chechnya. Whenever possible we visited hospitals because the suffering was so great there. Our IHF partners in the U.S. enabled us to bring relief supplies for patients and doctors. Of course, we could never bring enough to meet the overwhelming need, but we had committed ourselves to show people in Chechnya as much of the mercy of Christ as we could.

The IHF Maleka's Child program was named after Maleka, our manager's wife and the mother of six daughters.

In translation, Maleka means "Angel" and for her the name was a fitting one. From the first time I met her, she was genuinely committed to IHF's work. She was a great help to our mission and had a special place in her heart for her people in Chechnya.

Maleka was a joyful person, but there was one thing that made her life incomplete. It was that she had no son, and in an Islamic culture, a son is everything. Until a son was born, Maleka could only go from day to day hoping for this blessing from God.

In the summer of 2002, Maleka shared with us that she was pregnant. She specifically asked for us to pray that this child would be the son she had waited for.

We rejoiced with her and prayed that God would bless her with this request. The days flew by and soon it was time for her to deliver the child. She checked herself into Hospital #1 in downtown Grozny.

Joining the hundreds of other women in the same condition, Maleka trusted herself and her unborn child into the hands of God, and the women doctors at the clinic.

Soon, difficulties began to arise, however, and it was advised that a C-section would have to be preformed in order to save her and the life of the baby.

On a cold and dreary afternoon in late February 2003, Maleka drifted into a deep sleep under anesthetic gases. It would be almost two days before she would regain consciousness. When she did, her head hurt. The room she was in was silent and empty. There was no baby crying for its mother. She sensed something terrible had happened, just what, she didn't know.

A young nurse slipped into the room and then over to the bed where Maleka lay. With a sober face and tears in her eyes the young nurse informed Maleka that her baby had died during the operation.

"We tried everything we could, but our equipment malfunctioned. You and the baby were poisoned by too much anesthesia," she said.

Maleka lay silent, her heart broken, her eyes too swollen to cry. The crushing weight of the loss was too much to bear.

Later she found out that the baby was a boy. Idris had come and taken the baby away, and in traditional Islamic fashion had buried the body before the sun set that day. The only image Maleka saw of her precious baby boy was a simple Polaroid photo taken before the burial.

Maleka and Idris grieved the loss of their son - we grieved with them. In her heart, Maleka questioned God. She vowed to never set foot again in Hospital #1 in Grozny. The haunting memories of her tragedy were too much to bear.

Yet, through all of her grieving it seemed that God began to open her heart to the hope that one day she could see her son again. As a result of her loss, Maleka began to feel a renewed compassion for other Chechen women suffering from the same lack of proper medical care that had taken her son's life.

Maleka began to go back to Hospital #1 and visit the women there. We christened the IHF program to help these mothers and their babies "Maleka's Child" as a testimony to how God renewed Maleka's life in a time of heart-breaking loss.

This program was initiated to help supply special maternity care packages to women in the hospital who were waiting to give birth. Each package contained diapers, milk supplements, blankets, dry baby food and other needed hygiene products for the baby and the mother. We also made sure that gospel literature was included with each package as the women had a lot of time to read during their stay.

There was a practical and material benefit that our Maleka's Child care packages gave to the women and their newborns. However, for us, this was only one side of the blessing. Our hope was that not only would each woman have a safe and healthy baby, but that through the reading of God's word she would come to know Christ. After a woman left the hospital to return to her village or city, she would carry the scriptures and booklets with her, thus spreading the word of God into areas of Chechnya that were "no go" zones for us.

Through the financial support of individual donors and churches across America, IHF was able to purchase items in the local markets and assemble the Maleka's Child packages at our base in Gikalo. That saved us a lot of money in shipping costs.

There were times when members of a women's group at a church would personally quilt baby blankets and send them to our ministry office in Pennsylvania to be transported with us, then put in with our distributions. Several times we received boxes of handcrafted blankets from the ladies from Calvary Community Church in Phoenix, Arizona and Koinonia Fellowship in Rochester, New York, for example.

The care and love they put into each individual blanket was amazing, and the Chechen women loved the personal touch that it brought. Just knowing that Christian women in America cared about their plight opened their hearts to the love that flowed out of these simple gifts.

On one trip our heavily armored convoy of trucks and supplies pulled down the muddy lane that led into the courtyard of Grozny Hospital #1. Sidestepping the mud, I slipped into a white doctor's gown and pulled a little blue cap onto my head.

The title on my gown indicated I was a doctor of podiatry. There was irony in a podiatrist visiting pregnant women, I thought. I was not a doctor at all, nor were any of the other volunteers on our team. We had come to share our Maleka's Child program with hundreds of pregnant Chechen women who desperately needed medical care and support.

With packages in hand, we proceeded to enter the ward. Culturally, as a man, I would never have been allowed into such a facility. Even so, our team had been cleared to come inside and talk with each lady as we gave each a package.

It was a shock to me to see the conditions these precious ladies were living in.

Although some repair had taken place to the damage caused during the war, the conditions were still very poor for a woman in her final stage of pregnancy. At such a vulnerable time, when a woman would like to have some privacy, there was none. Each room was filled to capacity with women lying on single cots and sharing floor space. In one room alone I counted over fifty- five women. Nothing was secret or sacred here.

Food and any other supplies had to be brought in by relatives. Since it was wintertime, the only heat available in the entire building was an old wood stove near the end of the hallway. The walls were cracked and drafty.

Dampness was evident in many places, the perfect breeding ground for mold and mildew, hardly the kind of thing you want floating in the air in a maternity ward. At least the windows had panes.

At first, some of the ladies were shy and embarrassed to be seen by foreigners, especially by men. Some thought we were a U.N. group that had come to take pictures, write a report and then leave.

However, once the ladies saw that we were not there to make a circus of their plight they began to relax and talk to some of the women on our team. Some shared worry over the health of their baby, rarely their own heath. Their love and attention was always focused on their beloved babies.

Moving from room to room, handing out the care packages, we talked and prayed with the women.

In one particular room I felt led to address the entire room of women and share the gospel with them. This may have seemed a little intrusive because my hearers were a captive audience, yet I felt empowered by the Holy Spirit to speak. My message was a simple one, that Jesus himself came to earth as a little baby, and that his mother Mary didn't have the best of conditions to bring the Son of God into the world either.

After I finished sharing, a young lady stood in the back of the room. With tears flowing down her face she softly said, "Today is the first day since this horrible war began that someone has come to us and treated us like decent people. I had begun to think that everyone in the whole world had forgotten the Chechen people. I had come to believe that the entire world sees us as terrorists and bandits. Please thank your Christian friends in America for not forgetting us. Please let them know that we are not terrorists."

She had every reason to think Chechens were hated. We were in Chechnya just days after the horrible school tragedy at Beslan, Northern Ossetia. As the world watched in horror, Russian Special forces stormed the tiny elementary school where over 300 school children and teachers were being held hostage by what many claimed to be Chechen terrorists. Sadly, many children and teachers died in the botched rescue operation. To the world, all Chechens were now terrorists.

After the mayhem ended, only one terrorist was ever clearly identified as being Chechen. Rumors spread that the Ingushetians were involved; a gruesome payback for the loss of their children at the hands of Northern Ossetians in early 1991 during a regional conflict. Even more mysterious was how such a massive breach of security could have happened without local help and the local police being paid off. Grieving parents began to accuse local investigators of cover-up and conspiracy. The truth may never be known.

Maleka may have lost her son, but through IHF's Maleka's Child program, she was able to see her son live in hundreds of other moms and children in Chechnya.

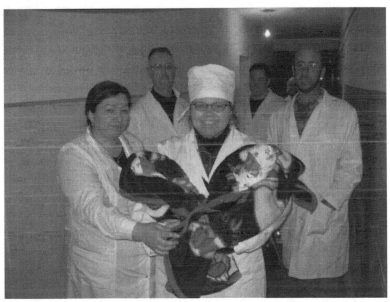

Helen and IHF Members – Maleka's Child Project

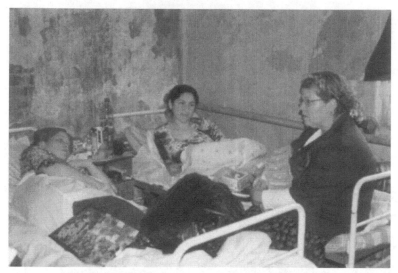

Helen with Chechen women – Maleka's Child Project

David with Chechen Mother & newborn – Maleka's Child Project

Chapter 11

Santa Claus is a Spy

Hugo is a jolly bearded man that comes from Schonaich, a small Black Forest village in southwestern Germany. He is in his late fifties, unmarried, and a Honeywell engineer by profession. We have traveled thousands of miles together sharing a common faith and sense of destiny.

I first met Hugo on an EEO trip to Russia's heartland in October 1992. From that first trip to now, God has connected us in spirit and in soul. To me he is a modern day apostle Paul and Saint Nicholas wrapped up in one. When I think of Hugo, I really do believe in Santa Claus.

Our bond is strange in that we live on two different continents, speak a different language, but have been connected by faith in God, and Lufthansa Airlines, to share the Gospel of Jesus Christ in some of the most interesting and unlikely places on earth.

Each morning we would start off the day with prayer and scripture reading. " *Danke Fatter,* " *sve zank thee fur dis dea.*" Hugo tried his best to pray in English to make me feel a part of it. I always enjoyed hearing him pray in Swebish, the native dialect for his part of Germany.

Hugo read from a little booklet that had been in his family for years, a devotional from C.H. Spurgeon. After this we would sing a Psalm and then pray again. I always enjoyed these mornings.

We shared many experiences in Chechnya. One of the more memorable ones came on a January day in 2004 during our

Christmas outreach to a Chechnya Children's Hospital just outside of Grozny.

Its director had invited our small IHF team to come and present our program to his children and their parents. The hospital was the only children's pediatric facility in the entire Chechen Republic.

Sultan, the director, was a well educated man and he was proud that he had been able to get his ward up and running without much help from Moscow or any other government office. He had befriended Idris and Maleka and had many questions about their involvement with Christians from America.

We would take gifts for each of the kids and their parents, as well as Bibles and other Christian booklets. With the familiar packing of trucks and loading clothing, food, and other needed supplies finished up, we were ready to head out.

Arriving at the hospital just before lunch, we were met by Sultan and one of his assistants. A white gown and a funny little blue shower cap were waiting for each of us. Even our feet needed to be covered.

We began bringing Christmas presents into the quiet and somber hallways of the hospital. The lady workers stared at us with puzzled looks on their faces. We were wearing the white robes but it was obvious that we weren't doctors. If we weren't doctors, then what were we doing in their ward causing trauma for children who were already dying?

Suddenly, out of nowhere, came a joyful man in red and white with black boots and a hat to match. It was Santa Claus!

The mood immediately swung into celebration and life. The moment had been seized. Hugo had saved the day. His eyes were twinkling and his cheeks were rosy. He was in his zone.

Excitement flooded the hallways of the hospital. You could hear the children giggling in their rooms. We went from room to room, Santa Claus leading the way.

Nurses and workers looked out of their rooms to see what was causing all the commotion. This scene reminded me of the movie "Patch Adams." When we dare to do things differently, God can use the smallest thing to show His love.

With a pull on his beard and a pinch of his cheek, Santa Claus was being used by God to bring hope back into these children's lives.

As Santa moved down the hallway, other members of our team came behind him to talk and pray with the children and their parents.

One of the team members, Sean, was a good friend and Missions Pastor at Rocky Mountain Calvary Chapel in Colorado Springs, Colorado. Sean and the RMCC congregation had supported IHF's work in Chechnya for many years. I had invited Sean to join us many times to see what God was doing through their support and prayers. Now, after many schedule adjustments, Sean was finally on the ground with us seeing the work firsthand.

Being a missionary at heart, Sean had traveled all over the world and had shared God's love with many people in need of help. However, on our trip through the streets of Grozny that morning, Sean leaned over to me and said, "David, I was in Kabul, Afghanistan last year. I saw firsthand the devastation of that city and its people. But seeing Chechnya and Grozny—I have to say I have never seen anything like this. How could something like this have happened in the 21th century? God have mercy."

Sean had echoed the words of philanthropist Fred Cuny, who had written in a report to the Soros Foundation before disappearing during the 1994-1996 Chechen war. He said, "Having been in Sarajevo and now Grozny during some of the worst fighting, I can say without reservation. Sarajevo was a picnic compared to this place. Grozny scares me."

Santa Claus had moved on to spread good cheer on the 2nd & 3rd floors. Remaining behind on the main floor, I saw Adam, one of our guards, standing in a doorway at the end of the hallway.

Walking towards him, I looked into a quiet side room to find Sean kneeling next to a little boy lying flat on his back with an I.V. in his arm. It appeared that Santa had overlooked this little room by mistake, and the young boy inside.

His mother held his hand. "My boy, Ahkmad, has severe nerve damage," she said with tears welling up in her eyes. "While giving birth, a bomb exploded near our house. Sultan and the doctors believe the shock from the explosion damaged his spine and nervous system. He is suffering from trauma and may never recover, he is alive, *In-sha-la*, but always in pain. They tell me in Germany they have sophisticated equipment that could possibly help him, but we can't go to Germany."

"May we pray for Ahkmad?" Sean asked.

The mother replie , "Of course, I am Muslim and I believe in God, but Allah hasn't answered. Since you are Christian, God maybe will hear you."

We prayed. The earth didn't move, but heaven did.

Leaving his room, I thought about her words. "OK, he can't go to Germany, so we'll bring Germany to him."

I ran upstairs, grabbed Santa Claus, and we headed back down to Akhmads' room to have a little fun.

Santa stepped into the room and immediately Akhmad's eyes lit up like a Christmas tree.

"Santa Claus," he called out.

A gleeful smile broke out across his face as Hugo's soft and tickly beard brushed across his nose and chin.

"God has answered your prayers!" his mother exclaimed.

Immediately, several other nurses came into the room. Seeing the joy on Akhmad's face, and his mother smiling, brought joy to them also.

Sultan joined us. It seemed his spirit was renewed as our visit was having a positive impact on the children and the parents in his hospital. Many parents were asking questions about the Children's Bibles we had given out and some asked for extra copies to give their friends.

Hugo communicated God's love to Ahkmad and the entire hospital that day in a simple way—by radiating the love of Christ. The Holy Spirit flowing out of him erased any barrier that language created. Our Santa didn't have a list of who was naughty or nice because it wasn't important. Hugo genuinely loved God's children and it didn't matter to him if he was German and this little boy was Chechen. Nationality had nothing to do with being God's servant or Santa Claus.

However, leaving the hospital that afternoon to return to our base at Lamb's Home, we experienced an event that demonstrated just how much nationality could affect our lives.

The trouble started as we traveled back through the center of Grozny on that late January afternoon. The shadows of night had already begun to fall as we hurried to get out of the city. It is hard enough to conceal the fact that you are a foreigner in Chechnya if you travel through the war zone with a military escort, but it is virtually impossible if border guards and renegades alike spot you because one of your group is wearing the "Big Red Suit" with a real beard to boot.

There was another thing that was likely to slow our exit from the city—Hugo as always was friendly with everyone he met, including Russian soldiers and border guards.

The last checkpoint we had to clear was the OMON post on the south side of town. Normally, this last post before getting to Gikalo is a friendly handshake between Idris and the Special Forces men that are stationed there and know him. But today it was different. The regular guards had been replaced with special GRU agents, members of Russia's Special Counter Intelligence Branch. This was not a good thing.

Hizir was driving the car ahead of us. Idris, Hugo and I were behind them in the van. Hizir was waved through without any problems.

I breathed a little easier until suddenly the guard stepped in front of our vehicle, pointed his automatic Kalashnikov at Idris and yelled, "STOP!"

Idris jumped out of the car and began yelling at the guard for holding his gun directly on us.

Before walking over to talk to the head officer, he motioned for us to stay quiet and not to make eye contact with the guards.

Before I could communicate this to Hugo in broken German, he opened the side door of the van and motioned the guards to come over and take a Bible and some chocolates, "Merry Christmas from Jesus and Santa Claus."

One of the younger guards started moving in our direction when the head officer yelled at him not to go near the van. They continued to hold us at gunpoint.

Although neither Hugo nor I could understand Russian well enough to know exactly what was happening, we both sensed something was desperately wrong.

A few moments later Idris came back and sat down in the van. Closing the door he nervously lit a cigarette and turned to Hugo and me and said, "If you know how to pray, you should pray. The GRU officer here believes that Hugo is a German journalist that the Russians have been looking for since he slipped across the Chechen border a few days ago. He is trying to contact the FSB to send agents to come and take us all to their interrogation station at Khankala. I am pleading our case that he is a German doctor who is visiting the Children's hospital in Grozny. He isn't buying my story."

This is the only time I have ever wished Hugo wasn't Santa Claus, or German.

We sat and prayed. *"Vater, Deine Ich Die Helfin"* (Father, you are our help), Hugo prayed in his Swebish (Black Forest) German dialect.

We both understood the trouble we were in. Most people who were taken to Khankala never came out, at least not in one piece. I didn't want to be on CNN.

The officer in the shed was yelling into his portable Motorola radio. Stepping outside, possibly to get better reception, he continued to yell into it, shaking it violently. There was no response. He continued to yell, but still no response. The FSB were not answering.

The officer became agitated with the situation, and Idris took advantage to press again for our release. The officer became more angry and started waving his arms and cursing at us. It was clear that he had been drinking and was not in complete control of his actions.

He threw the radio on the ground and commanded the guards to open the gate and allow us to leave.

"God answered your prayers," Idris shouted as we sped down the dark road toward Gikalo. "The FSB never heard the call from the officer."

We later learned from one of Idris' friends in the military what actually happened that day. The German journalist had never left Moscow but he had been detained at Sherymetyovo 2 International Airport. He was on assignment with Der Spiegel - Germany's equivalent of Time – to write a human rights abuse article on Chechnya. Evidently, Hugo fit his description perfectly, except for one thing, the "Big Red Suit." When the officer tried to contact the FSB, the batteries on the radio were dead. Santa Claus made it back to Germany.

Hugo has been an inspiration to me and many others over the years. I will always cherish his friendship and servant's heart for our work in Chechnya. This episode is just a small window into the many ways that he and I shared our lives together for the Chechen people. He has given of his time, money and life to share the gospel all around the world.

Our family visited Hugo at his home in *Schönaich* one Christmas on our way back from a missionary outreach in Turkey.

Our children were still young and being in Germany during Christmas time was enchanting.

Hugo's house fit the description of where you would expect him to live, a quiet little village nestled in the Black Forrest region of Southern Germany. "Silent Night" could have been written there. In fact, Schönaich means "beautiful night". It snowed the day our train arrived from Munich, making his village a winter wonderland. Hugo met us at the station wearing his signature red plaids and German hat.

During the few days we were there we reminisced about the adventures of faith we had taken over the years and talked about plans for future missions. Dottie and the children enjoyed walking around the village and visiting with Hugo's eighty-two year-old mother who lives in the same house.

My family and I have always had a childish wonderment about Hugo. He is such a generous human being and his appearance is much like the famous St. Nicholas. So last year, like in the classic

Christmas movie "Miracle on 34th Street," I asked him if he slept with his beard outside or under the covers.

With a twinkle in his eye and a tug on his beard he chuckled and said, "Outside the covers of course, the cold air makes it grow."

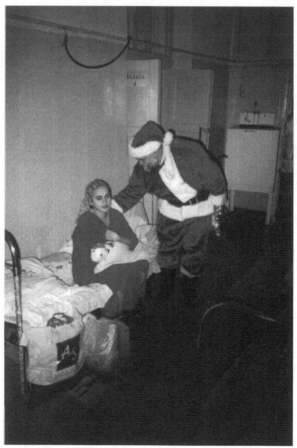

Hugo and Chechen mother with newborn

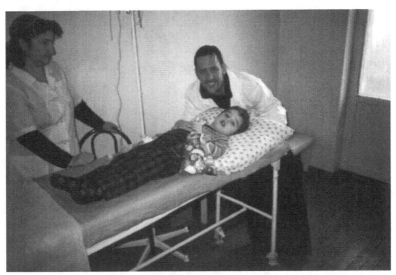

Sean and Akhmad

Hugo bringing cheer to children in hospital

Chapter 12

On Borrowed Time

Tony and Richard were two Christian brothers who came from Calvary Chapel, St. Petersburg Florida. Their church had sponsored over four hundred Christmas packages for IHF's Maleka's Child project. They joined our team and were now helping us distribute the gifts to Chechen moms and refugees in Grozny. The outreach went well but it didn't start that way.

Over my years as a missionary, anytime I get ready for a trip or outreach, things at home usually start going crazy. The car breaks down, pipes burst or a computer at our IHF office dies. It always seems to be this way.

However, in preparing for our January 2005 outreach, the scene was quiet—eerily quiet—until the last night before my departure. All that day I had a strange foreboding that this trip would be different.

I had no real reason to base my feelings on, just a gut feeling. I shared this with Helen, our West Coast IHF director, and she sensed the same thing.

We had made contact with Idris the day before to confirm all was well on the ground in Chechnya. Everything was arranged there for the trip and we had the green light from them. Everything was as good as possible, relatively speaking, for Chechnya.

The foreboding lingered all day. I talked with my wife Dottie about it and she comforted me saying that it was probably just exhaustion.

That evening our family gathered by the fireplace in our home. I wanted to pray with my wife and children since I would leave the next day. As we sat quietly praying, I heard a thump on our front porch door. At first, I thought "Who could that be at this time of the night?

I went to the door and opened it slowly. Stepping outside I looked around but saw no one. Then as I turned to come back inside, I looked down. Lying on its back was a black bird cold and lifeless.

At first I thought "What is a black bird doing flying around at night? I reached down to pick it up. It was cold and stiff. That's when a wave of fear swept over me.

I thought, "This bird has been dead for some time. It didn't fly into the door, it was thrown against it."

I am not superstitious, but my mind began to race with dark thoughts. Was this why I had the foreboding spirit? Was this a sign to come? Was the Lord trying to warn me and the team not to go into Chechnya this time?

I told Dottie and the kids about the bird and then went back and prayed more. The next day I left for Moscow.

In Moscow I met Helen, Tony and Richard. When we arrived it was bone cold. Hugo from Germany would meet us for the flight to Nalchik, a city in the Northern Caucasus, near Chechnya. There is only one flight per day so if you miss this flight you have to wait until the next day.

We arrived early at Knukovo, one of Moscow's regional airport hubs. There we waited for Hugo to arrive and then we all checked in for the flight. After security checks we walked upstairs and down the ancient corridor to the waiting room of the gate. It was around

6 p.m. and the temperature outside had plunged to near zero. Our flight would leave at 7:20 p.m., so we had time for tea.

Sipping on a scalding hot cup of tea inside the Knukovo airport is the same cultural experience as drinking a cup of espresso in Istanbul bazaar—you do both very carefully. You keep one eye on your belongings and the other eye on your neighbor. These domestic airports can be strange, dangerous and ethnically exotic places.

Even stranger are the airlines and the destinations they fly to in the former Soviet Union.

Virtually all fly ancient Ilyushin or Tupolev jets. Air Alania flies to Vladikavkaz, Northern Ossetia,. Karat Air goes to Nazran, Ingushetia. Air Elbrus—that's us—goes to Nalchik, capital of the Balkarian /Kharbadino Republic in Russia's Northern Caucasus region.

People of all ethnic diversities from the Northern Caucasus region were already sitting in the waiting room for the flight because Nalchik is a connecting point for people throughout that region. Tonight, four Americans and one German would add flavor to the mix as we were the only foreigners on board. No surprise.

The big surprise came in the form of the voice you would rather not hear. "Due to severe fog at the airport in Nalchik, we will delay our departure until 11 p.m.," the lady mumbled over the intercom. Was this another sign of a snake-bitten trip?

I had been here before. 11 p.m. turns into 2 a.m., and after that, it turns into a flight the next day.

The people in the waiting area reacted with a familiar moan and look of frustration.

Several hours went by and at 10:45 p.m. the lady came on the intercom once again and informed everyone that the fog hadn't lifted and that they would try again at 2 a.m.—though there was no guarantee.

That was all most people needed to hear and there was a mad dash away from the waiting area. Most people headed back to a friend or relatives' house in Moscow. Our houses were a little too far away for us to go back to.

The way I look at it, if God wanted that plane to fly at that time and in those conditions, it would have happened. However, if the pilot had not had enough rest, or if there is no visibility, I don't want my life to end by flying into the side of a mountain they couldn't see.

We grabbed a metal bench and each staked our claim. Elbrus Air isn't the kind of airline that provides free hotel vouchers. We were homeless and it was going to be a long cold night in the Knukovo airport.

At ten o'clock the next morning we flew the two hour, forty minute flight to Nalchik.

Idris was waiting at the airport, and so were others—Russian OMON troops. I had never seen this before in all of my years of flying into Nalchik.

Was this another sign of a trip that I should not have come on? Could it be my last? Between the five of us, we had 13 big duffle bags of gifts and clothing.

As we gathered our bags, we were questioned by one of the guards, "Why are you Americans coming to Nalchik?" "Why are you being picked up by Chechen people?"

We answered truthfully, "Because we like your city." He didn't seem amused, but he let us go. I am not sure why.

We were now almost a full day behind on our schedule. We couldn't get the police registration stamp in our passports since their offices were closed on the weekend. Idris shrugged it off and said we could get them on the way back. Only Moscow cared where you had been and who you had been with.

Also, being one day behind, all of our contacts and appointments in Chechnya would be compromised if we didn't make it into Gikalo that afternoon. We were to begin the outreach the next day.

It was around 1 p.m. when Idris decided to make a mad dash for Chechnya to get there before dark. Being on the road in Chechnya after dark is deadly, as I have said before. We had less than three hours before dark and it normally takes over four hours to drive this distance. Today would not be normal. In typical Idris fashion, we left Nalchik in a blaze for Grozny. Before long, our Volga car was streaking down the road at more than 180 kph—that's 110 mph—on bad tires. My prayer life became more fervent.

Our headlights soon lit up the road that turns towards Gikalo. I prayed as we approached the final checkpoint that we would not be mistaken for rebels and shot. The speed that Idris was traveling made us a prime target, but he was on a mission.

Huge lights were pointed at us as we came into the checkpoint. "Stop or we will shoot," the Russian soldiers yelled. Idris continued on.

Shots rang out in the air. I ducked down into the floor.

Skidding to a stop, Idris jumped out and yelled back at the guard to stop shooting. One of the officers recognized Idris and immediately things calmed down.

Idris apologized to the officer and explained that the car had a mechanical problem along the way and we had to repair it. After a few more tense minutes at the checkpoint we drove on down the road to Gikalo, Idris' home village.

God was gracious to us and we pulled into the little town under the cover of darkness. Tired and exhausted, we arrived at the compound of Lamb's Home. Normally, we would have been welcomed by excited children jumping up and down, but since we were late, they had already been put to bed.

Tonight the home was uncommonly quite. It seemed strange, like the life I knew here was gone. The same foreboding came over me. I didn't say anything to anyone but I sensed something was not right. Maybe I was just tired.

Idris was tired also. He left and went to his home around the block. Before leaving he gave our security guards instructions and our schedule for the following day. Adam and Bekhan were Chechen militia there to watch over us. They had been the security for me on almost every trip I had taken into Chechnya since the year 2000. They were loyal, and many times we had talked about the gospel and the teachings of Jesus.

Saying good night, we went upstairs to the room I had grown accustomed to over the years. The same room where on that fateful night in 2001, my family and eight other Americans were sleeping when all hell broke loose and gunfire had erupted in the street just outside of the home. Tonight, the guns were silent. It seemed peaceful—too peaceful. Had I become so familiar with the dangers that I didn't notice them anymore? Or was it as they say, "The calm before the storm."

Lying there in the dark on the wire mattress I thought again about the strange foreboding I had before coming. The dead black bird at my house the night before, the delay at Knukovo airport, the missing registration in our passports and today's close call at the military checkpoint.. There were always glitches in every trip, but it seemed like the entire trip had been one big glitch so far. I prayed that we had worked the bugs out and the next day would be better.

It seemed only minutes had gone by when I heard the giggling of the Lamb's Home children waking up to go to school. It was still dark, but breakfast was on in the dining room. Skipping across the courtyard in the cold morning air, the kids made their way to the kitchen for buckwheat and cheese. Soon they were off to school.

Our day would start with breakfast and then turn into a frenzy of work, preparing and packing humanitarian packages for women in maternity wards in Grozny.

After these visits we would depart for three huge apartment complexes at the edge of the city where hundreds of Chechen refugees had been packed into high-rises like sardines. This distribution was part of our Family to Family program, an outreach operated in tandem with Maleka's Child. Thanks to the generosity of our IHF partners, we had purchased enough oil, flour, cheese, and other basic commodities to feed over 500 families for a month.

The most important aspect of this opportunity was sitting down with families to share the gospel with them. We had brought the Chechen Gospel of Luke and several other pieces of Christian literature with us.

Filing into the buildings with our arms loaded down with packages and Bibles, we began giving the parcels to the families.

Maga, a young Christian man from Nalchik, volunteered to sit with the trucks and guard everything while we were taking packages to the families. He also organized the Bibles and the booklets that were being given to those receiving food parcels.

Our security guards, Adam and Aslanbek, jumped in to help while keeping a watchful eye on the team. With the buildings shaped in such a maze of hallways, it was impossible to guard us completely.

The air inside the building was thick—warm, humid and stale. I walked the hallways to see the reaction of the people receiving their parcels and Bibles. I especially wanted to talk to people about the Bible portions of Luke and the other booklets they had received. Many of them had questions about our faith and why we as Christians would risk coming to Chechnya to help Muslims.

After several hours of giving out the packages, we promised to return the following day. That turned out to be a big mistake.

The next day we showed up to finish our project. Two Central Asian men were standing near the door of the building smoking cigarettes. I could not tell if they were Dagestani or Kalmikyan, but I felt they were FSB agents, plain clothes men from Chechen Prime Minister Akhmad Kadyrov, the man who was currently in power.

The agents were not there the day before and I could feel ill intentions coming from their direction. We went through our same project procedures as before—unloaded the food packages from the trucks, placed Bibles and booklets into bags, then distributed them among the families in the building. The men watched us all afternoon. We should have never announced our intentions to return the next day. Someone had betrayed us to the FSB. We were now marked.

We finished our project before lunch and drove back to Gikalo. The children were out of school, and were waiting in the playroom to put on a New Year's program for us.

Exhausted from the mornings activities, the cooks gave us steaming cups of black tea to pep us up. After being out in the cold all day, the warm room was putting us to sleep, but the hot tea began to take effect. Our guards, Adam and Bekhan, had gone back to their militia post for the afternoon and would return after dark.

The kids from Lamb's Home looked like ice crystals wearing their Father Frost outfits. They usually held their New Year celebrations the first week in January and always liked to perform for guests. With songs, dances, poems and just plain fun, we were enjoying the children's program.

Suddenly Malka came running into the room with a fearful look on her face. Helen and I sensed something was wrong. Idris quickly left the room, motioning to us to stay quiet. The kids continued to sing. We weren't sure what was happening, but it soon became clear.

Walking into the playroom, the two men who had been watching us at the apartment building calmly came over and took a chair right next to me.

Malka hurried to get them hot tea and chocolates. Idris' face was beet red and sweat began to pop up on his forehead. Foreboding shadows swept over me again like a dark cloud. The FSB had not come to see the children's program. They had two armed agents with them and planned to stay awhile.

After a break in the program one of the agents leaned over toward me and in a smooth voice said "We would like to talk to you about your work and why you have come here to Chechnya."

The mixture of garlic and vodka on his breath was repulsive. It was the first time in all of the years that I had been coming to Chechnya that I would be questioned by the FSB. And not only me but Helen, Hugo and the other men that had come with us.

A young FSB agent came into the room wearing a black leather jacket and a Mhakarov pistol at his side.

"Sit down," he said. Thumbing through my passport he looked up and said, "We know you have come to Chechnya many times. You and your friends pose as Christians helping children and widows. Chechens are Muslims, not Christians. Who do you really work for? The CIA, NSA? My mind flashed back to years before at the opening day ceremony when I had sat across from one of the head FSB men from Grozny. This time was different. I was being interrogated.

"You answered your question already," I replied. "We are Christians and we come in the name of Jesus Christ to share His love and hope with the Chechen people."

Looking up we made eye contact. His eyes were dark and sinister.

Idris chimed in and tried his best to validate us with our official Lamb's Home paperwork and our permission papers from the regional offices in Grozny, but these guys weren't interested.

The young man questioned all of us that afternoon, and after some time he left the room. He also took written statements from each of us stating that we were violating sovereign Russian soil by not having official permission from "his" superiors in Grozny to be on Chechen land.

His buddies were busy copying all of our information from our passports and visas. I am not sure how long we were in the room with him but it seemed like hours.

Waiting, waiting—darkness soon fell over Gikalo. Deep down, I was afraid that we would all be taken in to Khankala, the Russian military base, for further questioning. However, my gut feeling was these guys were not official Russian FSB, but were intent on something much more sinister. They were mercenaries, I felt, entrepreneurs in human trafficking.

We were in trouble. Now, the shadows of foreboding were more than just shadows, they had become reality. For years I had come to Chechnya, and by God's protection, had returned to my family and friends in America. Tonight, for the very first time, I wasn't so sure that we would make it back. I remembered my first trip to Gikalo in 2000 when I thought that I was being kidnapped by Chechen rebels. That turned out to be just hysteria on my part. Tonight, I was face-to-face with those fears again, and this time it really could be happening.

The agent returned to the room and gave our passports back. Without a word, he turned and walked out, joining his fellow agents in the courtyard below.

Idris went down with him, playing along with their conversation, trying to figure out what their next move would be. After smoking a few cigarettes, they assured Idris not to worry, the Americans would be well. It was almost 8 p.m. when the FSB agents disappeared through the green gates of Lamb's Home into the dark Chechen night. I felt we hadn't seen the last of them.

Collapsing onto the bed, I became physically sick from the nights events. Tony and Richard came up and prayed with me. Fear had gripped me like an iron hand and it seemed like a claw was digging into my heart. My legs felt heavy and wouldn't move properly. Darkness was closing in on all sides. My mind began to entertain fatal thoughts. I felt trapped. Questions began to haunt me. What if those thugs came back? What would we do? Were they finished with us or was this just a ploy to lull us into a false security?

It was after midnight when I heard a knocking at the Lamb's Home gate. Our guards, Adam and Bekhan, had returned after the FSB incident and were on watch.

Fog hung low in the street and the village was quiet, except for the distant barking of dogs somewhere out in the field. I could see Adam open the gate and a stranger stepped inside. They talked for a few minutes and then just as mysteriously as the stranger had come, he left. The message had been delivered.

The message was a simple one—the Americans must get out of Gikalo before 8 a.m. or things will not be good for them or Idris' family. The agents who had been there the night before were coming back, this time with reinforcements to take the Americans back to Khankala, the Russian detention camp for Chechen rebels. Those taken to this camp were rarely ever seen again.

Idris came to the home early in the morning rushing everyone to get ready to leave. Like being let down over the wall in the basket or deliverance from the snare of the fowler, this was God's way of protecting us from the enemy who would have loved to cause us bodily harm and torture our families. God's miraculous salvation was once again being played out right before my eyes. Grabbing our bags we left just as the sun began to rise over the mountains in the East.

As we sped out of the village and out of Chechnya that morning, my heart raced. We had worked with total openness for over six years in the Republic. During those times we had close calls with the military and navigated many security situations, but nothing this sinister. All the way out of Chechnya, I feared we would be detained by the police or FSB at any checkpoint.

Maybe those men were real agents and they had reported our departure ahead with orders to detain us. Maybe they would stop us at the airport in Nalchik, while boarding our flight back to Moscow. It could even happen the next day at Sheremetyovo International Airport in Moscow as I left for the U.S.

Those fears were never realized. We did make it home. However, what happened that night made me face the reality that after years of work in Chechnya, the sands in our hourglass were running out. We were on borrowed time.

David with Chechen Militia guards Adam, Bekhan and Vacha

Chapter 13

The Mountains of God

As legend has it, the Caucasus Mountains are where God walked with Adam and Eve. It is the also the location of the highest peak in Europe, Mt. Elbrus.

Located in the Republic of Kharbadino-Balkaria, Russia, Mt. Elbrus was the winter playground for the elite of the communist party in the old Soviet Union. With year round snow skiing and natural sulfur hot spring spas, travelers from as far away as Eastern Europe, Turkey, Iran, and Iraq came to play in this wild and exotic region.

After the fall of the Iron Curtain and the resurgence of the regional ethnic wars that sprang up in the Caucasus during the early 1990's, tourism dwindled as fear increased.

Now, a decade later, life was returning to normal and Elbrus was once again calling. In the summer, mountain climbing teams from all around the world would attempt to ascend the snow covered peak. From May until late August it was common to find teams from Germany, the Czech Republic, Poland and Ukraine trekking across the glaciers and ravines of these rugged peaks.

Mt. Elbrus was also where we held Lamb's Home children's summer camps. With school finished by the end of May, all of the children looked forward to leaving Chechnya and spending the majority of their summer in the mountains. Being able to leave the environment of war and the tragedies that had ripped their innocence from them was a wonderful experience for each child.

Besides, the air was clean, there were no guns firing at night, and raging rivers of ice cold snow melt and mountain glaciers were the perfect place for teams of Christian volunteers to come and work with the orphan children IHF was caring for.

It was next to impossible to find a camp in the mountains that would lease space to us—no one could believe that Americans, let alone Christians, would be working with Chechen Muslims.

Post 9/11-era phobias ran deep. Sinister suspicions haunted us, especially since we were harboring "five year-old orphan bandits" from Grozny. Idris had many contacts all over the region but finding someone to allow us to conduct a Christian camp for the kids from Lamb's Home proved harder to do than we ever imagined.

One day in late April 2002, Idris and I had met a Kharbodinian man named Bandar. He was a man who seemed to have a compassionate spirit towards the plight of the Chechen people, especially the kids. He owned a small campground near Mt. Elbrus. The facilities were nothing fancy, but adequate— and most importantly, he was open to having Chechen kids stay there.

Bandar was nice, but he knew that we were a foreign organization and he smelled money. After all, he didn't drive a black Mercedes by having compassion on orphans. He was a business man first, a humanitarian second—or third, depending upon the deal to be made. Being American in a foreign land has its positives, but it also comes at a price much of the time. Our agreement was settled on a hand shake. Idris would bring the children to Bandar's camp. He would charge us a price for the kids, and a special price for the Americans that would come.

After meeting Bandar, we decided to take a ride up to his camp and check out the facilities ourselves. It was a two hour drive from

Nalchik to Mt. Elbrus. The two lane road snaked its way up through the ancient valleys of the Balkarian plain traveling over the same ground that Alexander the Great traversed during his march of conquest there.

From the rolling foothills the road is quickly swallowed by towering cliffs and mountains that are home to only eagles and mountain sheep. Rushing torrents of ice and snow melt from the glaciers of Kazbeck and Elbrus crash wildly down the valley in a cascade of water, cutting through gorges of granite and over boulders the size of cars. It is beautifully wild and untamed, God's raw power displayed.

There are a couple of villages that you pass along the road as you go up to Bandar's camp. These villages live and die by the tourists that come from Europe and Russia to climb Mt. Elbrus.

Nestled just before the base of Mt. Elbrus is a little village called Cheget. With a decent hotel and ski lift onto one of the surrounding mountains, it is a magnet for skiers and snowboarders. It also has a great little outdoor market for buying local woolen materials such as socks, sweaters, hats and rugs. The local shepherds bring their wool to this market and the women weave it into all kinds of articles.

It was afternoon by the time we arrived at Bandar's camp. Even though it was April, the mountains had not warmed up that much. Walking over the grounds we drank in the cool mountain air.

The camp was simple, a three-story A-frame lodge with a kitchen, a playground, a nearby river and hiking trails – perfect for us.

As we prepared to leave, I noticed a pole with a dinner bell on it near the front of the lodge. Walking over to the bell I saw it was inscribed with something in German. Upon closer inspection I realized it was the verse from Matthew 11: " *Come unto me all you who are heavy laden and I will give you rest.*" I recalled the fish bricks that were in the walls at Lamb's Home. It seemed that the Lord was giving me another sign that we were in the right place at the right time.

The camp program we wanted to give the kids was to give them a time of rest and peace. The mountains of Mt. Elbrus were the place to provide this. Without the fear and sounds of guns and rockets exploding, the children could make a step toward emotional health. Bandar's camp would be a place of rest for them.

The sun had slipped behind the mountains by the time we came down from the camp to the main road. Hungry, we decided to go back up to Cheget and have a meal of *shoshleek* and *plimini* before traveling back to Nalchik.

In the mountains, the taste of lamb seems to have more flavor than in the lowlands. It has to be the high altitude, clean water and grass, I suppose. There, on that early Spring evening, we sat on the patio of a little stone walled restaurant, ate freshly cooked lamb, and watched the full moon rise over the snow covered peak of Mt. Elbrus.

That summer we returned and held our first Lamb's Home camp at Bandar's camp on Mt. Elbrus, one of four we were able to have over the years. Transporting the kids out of Chechnya for the summer was a wonderful way to heal their psychological and emotional wounds. It also allowed us to share the gospel with them through children's Bible stories and games. The beautiful mountain environment also provided our Lamb's Home workers with a much needed getaway.

Having traveled from Nalchik that morning, our American team arrived at the camp by noon as we had planned. Idris and the bus carrying the thirty-eight children from Lamb's Home would arrive later on that evening, Lord willing. It was only a seven hour drive from the Chechen Republic but the real factor was—if all went well.

The war in Chechnya had caused many problems for Chechen people. Traveling in and out of the Republic was a major hassle. Bringing an entire bus load of Chechen children was a really big deal. Having to cross several regional borders in Ingushetia, Northern Ossetia, and then Kharbadino/ Balkaria, the road these children would travel to get to the camp would be long and trying.

The afternoon passed, but there was no busload of excited children. Afternoon turned into early evening, then into night. There were no phone calls from Idris or any of the workers connected with the caravan. It was well past the time that they should have arrived. Some of us sat on the steps of the lodge waiting to hear traffic coming up the hill.

The stars in the pitch black night of the summer evening seemed close enough to touch. The only sound to be heard was the river rushing down the valley nearby. What could have happened? Did the bus break down? Was there a problem leaving the Chechen republic? Had they been detained at some border along the way? We didn't know.

Around midnight we heard the sounds of a bus coming up the road. Our workers ran outside to meet Idris and the children. It was a delight to hear the high pitched voices of the children reverberate through the crisp night air. They had finally arrived at the camp, almost 10 hours late. The ordeal they had endured that day began to unfold through the frustrated voice of Idris and the others.

"We've been detained at the Northern Ossetia border for over 7 hours!" Idris grumbled.

"All of our paperwork was in order and yet the Northern Ossetian border guards refused to allow us to pass until we paid them a bribe. I refused to do it. They made all of the kids get off the bus and stand on the side of the road! They wouldn't allow any of them to go to the toilet, so I just told the kids to pee right on the road. I threatened to call a friend at the local newspaper to come and report this terrible injustice that was being done to our children. This scared them and they finally let us go. It is only because they are Chechen that they are treated this way!"

Unfortunately, Idris was right. The war had made Chechen people an unwanted group within the Northern Caucasus region. The reputation of being bandits and terrorists had unfortunately been transferred onto the children as well. Not only did this make it difficult to find a camp for Chechen children, but it also made getting there difficult.

It was all very degrading for the children, and I prayed that the ordeal would not have a permanent effect on them. The exhausting day over, it was not difficult to get their tired little bodies to sleep.

The next day dawned with an air of excitement and anticipation. The sounds of happy children's voices echoed off of the hillside of the camp. Camp workers rang the Matthew 11 bell to signify that breakfast was being served. They marched in single file holding hands and with wide smiles across their faces. The children from Lamb's Home had finally arrived. The trials of the day before were distant memories by now and it seemed that the kids had totally forgotten that anything had even happened.

After breakfast our team organized games and spent the morning laughing with the children in the freedom of the peaceful atmosphere that the mountains provided. Here there was no danger of war and turmoil. No bombed out buildings to see, only green trees and rushing waterfalls. The only things flying overhead were eagles soaring high above the snow capped mountains. God had created such a wonderful place for us to share His love with the kids from Chechnya.

After lunch, the children had a short nap time while our team prepared a Bible story and crafts to illustrate the story. What a joy it was to share stories from God's Word and see a group of children react, hearing them for the first time ever.

That day, the story would be about how God makes all things new. The team had prepared a live re-enactment of the stages a butterfly goes through to become a butterfly. Complete with a person hanging from a tree, they acted out the stages of metamorphosis. The worm, cocoon and the finished butterfly! As the story literally unfolded before their eyes, the children were mesmerized to see how God can take the ugliest worm and transform it into a beautiful creature through the regenerating power of Jesus Christ. Our summer camps at Mt. Elbrus provided an opportunity for the children to see God's awesome beauty displayed through nature.

As part of our camp experience, we designated one day to enjoy some of this wild beauty. My favorite thing to do, and the one I suggested strongly to everyone, was to join with us in taking the cable trams up to the 17,985 feet base camp of Mt. Elbrus. Even if a person was faint-hearted or scared of heights, I tried my best to convince them to go. Most people took my advice, even my wife.

As the highest peak in Europe, the view was breathtaking. On a clear day, you could actually see from the Black Sea, where the range starts, eastward toward the southern tips of Chechnya, and then to the border of Azerbaijan and the Caspian Sea.

The last camp we held was in August 2005, the trip up to the base camp of Mt. Elbrus was the most memorable, since I had Dottie and my children with me.

It was fitting that they would be there on this trip, as they had been on the initial trip when we opened our children's home in Chechnya. Full circle, as it turned out, they would be with me at our last IHF camp at Mt. Elbrus.

There were several others on the team, including Hugo from Germany. He had been at every camp we had conducted, so it was appropriate that he too be here for the last ride up the hill.

We arrived at the little village of Elbrus just before lunch, and the warm sun was reflecting a brilliant white glare off of the snow covered peaks surrounding the valley. Even in late August, the weather can be fickle here at this altitude. Getting a crystal clear day is a true blessing from God.

I had been on this adventure before when it looked favorable, only to get half way up the mountain and the weather change. Clouds could roll in quickly, fog obscure the view of the peaks, and it can snow at the drop of a hat.

Today, however, there wasn't a cloud in sight. The sky was so blue it resembled a sapphire on snow. My prayers were answered. I had told everyone how beautiful the ride up the mountain was going to be. Now, they would see for themselves. My kids were excited. My wife—well, I'll explain later.

Weaving our way through the maze of stalls around the tram area, we came to the little booth to purchase our $10 round trip per person fare up the mountain. A large tram took you up to almost 16,500 ft. The last thousand feet or so up to the base camp was a very simple single person ski-lift chair. Dottie was fine knowing about the large tram. It was the last little detail about the chair that I didn't share with her.

The huge steel cables carrying the tram for the first leg up the base of the mountain vibrated with a high pitch hum. The massive wheel turning in the wooden tram house was old and rusty, but it worked. The massive *canatka*, or gondola, held twenty people comfortably. With tickets in hand we waited as the tram bringing people down the mountain slowly entered the wheelhouse.

Teenagers from Nalchik with snowboards, a couple on a romantic getaway, tourist from Armenia, hikers from Czechoslovakia—the tram was an international potpourri of people. With the group of Americans and Hugo from Germany added in, people on the tram seemed to have a heightened sense of cheerfulness.

Hugo was always friendly and wanted people to know why he was so full of joy. It was because God had put a love for them in Hugo's heart. He always wanted people to hear the Good News of Jesus Christ. He was a modern day apostle Paul.

The tram quietly and effortlessly ascended up the mountain. Looking out the window, the view was breathtaking. Patches of bright green grass and highland wildflowers graced the landscape of brown and black decomposed granite.

Having left the tree line already, the blue-white glaciers that cover much of the surrounding mountains began to come into view. Like majestic icebergs they seemed to float on an ocean of snow.

Suddenly, our tram jolted to a stop. Transfixed on the beauty of the ride, we had come to the first station house without me even noticing it. We got off and transferred to the next tram.

Leaving the second wheelhouse the view became even more incredible. Looking straight ahead, the two peaks of Elbrus were now visible, the lesser one on the left.

Towering into the deep blue sky on the right side, the main snow covered summit of Mt. Elbrus touched the heavens. Unlike many of the other high peaks of the world, Elbrus has very few other peaks to shadow it, making it all the more impressive and majestic. It is not hard to believe that God once walked here. At least today He was here. I felt closer the higher we went.

The air was getting thinner and noises less audible. The click of the cable wheels was the only intrusion. Hugo, and everyone else had stopped talking. It almost seemed that we were entering a holy realm where reverence should be given.

The tram neared the second wheelhouse and began to slow to a mere crawl. Stepping out onto the landing, we walked over to the lift chair station. Dottie looked at me and asked where the last tram was. Things got a little dicey from here out.

The thought of being in mid-air, sitting on a little metal chair, suspended by a steel cable at 17,000 feet did not impress her at all. But being the champion she is, she got in line with everybody else and before she could say "Hail Mary," the chair swept her up and away.

I grabbed the next chair and soon we were climbing upward towards the base camp. Being alone on the chair, feet dangling, silently gliding, at moments just a few feet over massive black lava rocks, the serene feeling of being near to God was strong.

Slowly, steadily, like floating in space, the ride to the base camp was amazing. Now, just a few more yards and the chair would spit us out at base camp Mt. Elbrus, 17,985 feet above sea level.

At the base camp were a dozen old fuel tanks that were converted into housing for climbing teams attempting to reach the summit. Teams from Ireland, Czechoslovakia, Russia, Ukraine and Italy were there, some with high tech equipment, some with basic gear. We heard that just two days before our arrival, a team from Poland had lost two climbers, who had fallen to their deaths through an ice fissure. Mt. Elbrus is beautiful but it also is dangerous.

One climber Hugo and I spoke with was going down the mountain due to altitude sickness. He had tried unsuccessfully to reach the summit the day before, but a couple hundred meters below the summit his body shut down and he became very ill. I learned from him that acclimating to the altitude is one of the hardest things to do and is one of the leading causes in fatalities among climbers. "I'll be back, in a little better shape next time," he said.

It seemed the Lord spoke to me through the climber's words that we also had to adjust to many new altitudes in life. Our spiritual climb can be very dangerous if we don't take the time to wait on the Lord to acclimate to our surroundings.

Getting to the base camp was only half of the fun for me. As was our custom from previous trips, Hugo and I brought a special picnic lunch to share with those tram members who joined us. The picnic lunch that day on Mt. Elbrus was one of those meals that you never forget.

Mt. Elbrus is where we were able to spend quality time with the orphan children and our Chechen staff in a setting that was relaxed and tranquil. Our team took hiking adventures up glaciers and across international borders in those mountains. We spent hours under the stars around campfires, roasting marshmallows and lamb, and sharing Bible stories by the roaring rivers. We experienced the presence of God under the trees of this special place.

Children hear Bible stories

Lambs Home kids and staff – Mt. Elbrus

Chechen Lambs Home Staff with Bibles – Summer Camp – Mt. Elbrus

David and Hugo – Mt. Elbrus – Russia

Chapter 14

Seeds of Hope

IHF's work in Chechnya existed during the volatile time period from 1997-2006. By that time two brutal wars had ripped the life and soul out of the innocent people of this tiny Republic in Russia's Northern Caucasus. Thousands of Russians and Chechens had died, maybe tens of thousands, no one knows for sure.

From my first border crossing in 1997, until my final trip in March 2006, I had crossed the Chechen border over 20 times, with the majority of those happening between 2001 and 2005. Each time could have been my last time, but God was gracious and He covered me with His grace and mercy.

I had come back from Mt. Elbrus with the cold reality sinking in that our season of ministry in Chechnya was coming to an end. That day we had come down from our picnic on Mt. Elbrus, our team, including Idris and Maleka, Dottie, Helen and Hugo, had sat around a table and discussed the future. It became clear to me then that events were enveloping us and we needed to revaluate our work in Chechnya.

God had opened the door for us to go and plow and plant the seeds of His gospel in the hearts of the Chechen people, and now it appeared He was closing that field. Our ministry had always held the position that when security issues became so bad that we couldn't travel into the Republic and effectively share God's love, we would take that as God's sign to leave. It appeared our work would soon be over there.

It was not just about my own safety or that of our teams; these same issues plagued Idris and Maleka too. They were under the constant scrutiny from local FSB and others who wanted to exploit them for money. They knew that IHF was sponsoring Lamb's Home and that gave them the advantage to pressure Idris to pay more "fees," as they called it, to allow the home to operate. We called it extortion, of course, because that was what it was.

Hizer had left Lamb's Home due to family concerns, leaving Idris and Maleka to manage day-to-day operations. This was not Idris' strength and soon the stress began to take its toll on him emotionally and physically. Just before our camp in the summer of 2005, he suffered a mild heart attack and was in the hospital for several weeks.

Maleka tried her best to hold things together, but it was impossible for her to do her own work and Idris' too. Idris had special skills when it came to working with border guards and officials, and with him out of commission, we were severely crippled. In Chechnya, dealing with FSB agents and Chechen officials was not a woman's job.

At the same time Malka, Maleka's sister, our main cook on whom we depended so much, told us she was trying to get refugee status in Germany and would emigrate as soon as possible.

Several other members of our Lamb's Home staff left for different reasons and it seemed that the once vibrant community of workers we had at the start was beginning to fade away.

Trying to manage things from America was becoming very difficult for me and our IHF staff. Everyone agreed that the security situations had become so bad in the Republic that it was time to consider closing the work and the children's home itself. It was decided that we would continue the Maleka's Child program through the Winter of 2005-2006, and then begin to try to place the children at Lamb's Home with loving Chechen families.

Idris and Maleka started to find permanent homes for the kids at Lamb's Home and finish the Maleka's Child distributions. We continued to support the children's home on an interim basis. After the kids finished their school year, IHF would discontinue its work in Chechnya for good. In the Bible, *Ecclesiastes* says there is a time and season for everything under the sun., including a time to start and a time to end.

The Fall of 2005 was a difficult time for me and IHF, yet God's hand was in all that was happening. Even though we had committed to continue supporting the children's home and our workers through the Spring of 2006, it felt as though we had lost a family member and in my heart I began grieving the loss.

Adding sorrow to this, some of the decisions that had been made regarding our work in Chechnya had been misunderstood by some ministry partners, thus adding to the unbelievable emotional spiral that I went into during those days. My family and I were dealing with issues that seemed to imply that God had thrust us into a perfect storm. I spent a long and cold winter trying to find balance to life and God's purposes in all that was happening. Yet, God was faithful and His purposes continued to unfold.

Many decisions had been made and many remained. By February, 2006, I boarded a plane and headed back to Chechnya. It was the trip I feared would come. Helen and I would make our final trip to see Idris and Maleka, our final trip to Lamb's Home, and our final trip into Chechnya. By God's grace, it would be our final trip out. It was the hardest trip of my life.

Maleka was at our IHF apartment. Food was waiting, chicken, pickled cucumbers, garlic, bread – but this time, the food was not as good. Nothing seemed to be the same. Our hearts were heavy. The next day, Idris came, and just like many times before, we made our final dash down the M29 into Chechnya. This time the trip was somber. Idris didn't talk much but, as usual, he drove like a maniac. There weren't as many checkpoints and those we did encounter were easier to pass through. Things seemed better, more traffic, more roadside markets.

It was gray and cold in Gikalo when we arrived that afternoon. The gates of Lamb's Home were shut. Things seemed quiet. The excitement and thrill of the children running out to meet us was missing, most had not yet returned from school. Even so, one of the boys, Ramzan came running out and threw his arms around our necks.

"Hello David, Hello Helen, my English good?" he asked, grinning from ear to ear. He had mastered this greeting and wanted to show off for us.

Malka came out of the kitchen with her sweet smile. She knew this would be our last time for fellowship. Tears were already welling up in her eyes.

Lida had taken over managing the home now that Hizir was no longer there. With her kind disposition and care, she was doing the best she could, but in Chechnya, authority is a man's world. She was well qualified and capable, just in the wrong world.

The children returned, but there were fewer than usual. Idris had already begun to place some kids with extended families as we had asked him to do. His major problem would be placing a family of five brothers.

That afternoon we spent time talking with the kids and sharing tea with the workers. It wasn't the same though, everyone knew what was happening. The glory had left Lamb's Home.

That evening we spent the night at Idris and Maleka's home for security reasons. We had not secured any armed guards and Idris had been warned that there were those in the village that knew we had come. Whatever this meant, Idris and I took it as a warning to stay secluded – we felt the Lord had given us intelligence that was valid and credible and that we should take it seriously. We also decided that it would be best for us to leave early the next morning – how fitting to end the way it had begun years before.

Maleka prepared a full table of *gigi* galish that night. We laughed as we remembered that she had prepared the same meal for me the first time I met her and Idris when they were refugees and living in Nazran, Ingushetia, in 1999. I guess it was her way of bringing things full circle.

After dinner, we sat together and worked out some final details that needed to take place with the closing of the home and our work. It was not as easy time. I remember Idris being distant and avoiding any direct engagement. I think he just wished everything would work out and that no one would get their feelings hurt, including his.

As a Chechen man, he was not supposed to show any weakness, even if he felt like it.

At one point he slapped me on my knee and in a typical male way, sighed and said, "David, you have been a good friend and example to us. God bless you for all your help to the Chechen people and our family." And with that he got up and left the room.

That was the last real eye-to- eye contact that we had. It seemed so quick, so final. We had lived our lives together for the past five years, shared bread together, dodged bullets together, escaped kidnappings together—and God knows what else. Now he was gone, just like that.

It was freezing in Idris' house. I slept with every stitch of clothes I had. It didn't help. I never got warm and sleeping was impossible. Lying awake all night, I had a lot of time to reflect. After nine years of travel and sharing the gospel in Chechnya, the work was coming to a close. My heart was breaking, aching, dying. It seemed we had only started, but now I was facing a harsh reality. What God had birthed, He would continue, but without us.

Like a night of old family movies, my mind began the picture show. Scenes of sharing our Christian lives with the Muslims in Chechnya. Times we had laughed together, cried together, feared together, and rejoiced together. Seeing little Chechen children find such joy and hope in watching Hugo dance around in his Santa suit during our Christmas parties at Lamb's Home. The times we would watch the kids light up like Christmas trees as they pulled new pajamas and presents of dolls and little metal cars from their gifts from America. The times when we would tell them about Jesus being born as a little baby in a manger, and one of the children asking if Jesus wore diapers like other little babies.

My mind went back to times of sitting out back at Lamb's Home, roasting skewers of lamb over an open fire while Russian artillery flew overhead hitting Shatoi, an infamous mountain stronghold for Chechen rebels.

I remembered the orange glow of the night sky, illuminated by the burning oil well fire on the hilltop just above the village of Gikalo.

I remembered the times we sat up late into the night, discussing the Bible with our Chechen militia security guards. They were angels of mercy .

I remembered the sleepless hours, wondering if we were making a difference in the hearts of the Chechen people. There were hours of faith, hours of doubt and hours of prayer.

The movies in my mind continued. I began to visualize the faces of thousands of women that we had blessed through our Maleka's Child program. Faces of babies we had saved through a simple program supplying milk and diapers. Babies delivered healthy, warm and cared for.

I wondered if their mother's hearts were warmed by reading the Bibles we gave them? Would a child one day ask its mother where the beautiful blanket came from that had the Bible verse sewn onto it? Would its mother tell them about the day during the war that a group of Christians came and gave them that special gift to help save their life? God knows. I hoped we caused them to feel loved, like God wanted them to feel.

The progression into the next set of pictures in my mind was natural. From the bombed out maternity wards of downtown Grozny, to the Muslim families we helped through our Family to Family outreach. As a branch of Maleka's Child, we began going into run down apartment blocks in Grozny, supplying food parcels to hundreds of refugee families that had been forced back into the Chechen republic after the U.N. and Russian camps had been closed in Ingushetia.

Tragically, this produced another humanitarian nightmare for the Chechen people, but for us, another opportunity to share God's love. There we were in those movies in my mind, food parcels and aid, sharing the gospel in practical ways—Bibles being distributed all over Grozny by a German with a heart like the Apostle Paul and Christians from America who wanted to make a difference.

I thought about those 15,000 copies of the Chechen Gospels of Luke that we had printed by faith, and which we had seen distributed throughout Chechnya. Hopefully they found their way into the hearts and hands of the thousands of Chechen refugee families we helped in the U.N. camps of Ingushetia.

I know for sure that over a thousand desperate families in the bombed out and besieged village of Komsomskaya received their personal copy because I personally handed each one a copy that day. Thousands of others had been given out during hospital visits, Christmas outreaches and humanitarian aid distributions. Like planting sugar in an ant hill, God's Word had been distributed all over the Chechen republic. I rejoiced to hear the Lord say, " *My Word will not return void but will accomplish all that I intend for it.*"

Lamb's Home and IHF's work existed in Chechnya for almost ten years. It was supported solely through the sacrificial gifts and efforts of Christians of all denominations. We never assumed that it would be an easy thing to do. In fact, we knew very little of what we were getting into when we first started. Even so, God gave us a wonderful window of time to care for the Chechen people and share the love of God with them.

From the time we officially opened Lamb's Home on September 1, 2001, until its closing in June 2006, hundreds of Chechen children passed through its doors, each with their own horror story. Each left with their own miracle.

I once heard about a young man from England who died while serving on the mission field. As his father went through his personal belongings he came across a line his son had written in his Bible, "No reserves...no retreats...no regrets."

Jesus spoke about a kernel of wheat that must fall into the ground and be buried before it brings forth fruit. In Chechnya, I believe we did that—we buried ourselves. Buried where? In the hearts of Chechen orphans, in mother's wombs, in refugee's mouths, in the minds of Muslim elders, in the gun sights of Russian soldiers, in FSB files, on Mt. Elbrus, and in the blood stained streets of Grozny. I have faith that the seeds have sprouted.

Lambs Home Workers

Chapter 15

Beauty From Ashes

I have read of men and women that spent their entire lives plowing and planting the message of Jesus Christ in areas where the soil is hard. In the Bible, Jeremiah never saw one convert during his ministry.

A missionary named David Livingstone spent 20 years in Africa before seeing any fruit for his labor.

Hudson Taylor died in China before he ever saw the great outpouring of God's Spirit on the Chinese.

In our Western culture, success is often judged by outward results and numbers. I do not believe this is God's way of looking at things. He looks at people's hearts, and from our human perspective we'd never be able to get the numbers to tally.

To say that we saw thousands come to Christ in Chechnya would not be accurate—we didn't. But we did see the gospel touch hearts in eternal ways. The one-on-one encounters we had meant more to me than anything. If just one of those precious Chechen souls truly grasped the gospel and it took root, then God can reach the entire Chechen population through their witness. God's hand touched many people, and we believe there will be a harvest in due season.

After sharing nine years of tears and joy with them, it is hard to forget their faces. There is not a day that goes by that I don't think about our friends there and pray for them.

Included in my prayers is Kiem, the mullah of Gikalo. This man was the head teacher in the village. My first meeting with him was to obtain permission for us to work in the village. Without this we would not have been able to operate Lamb's Home. On many occasions I sat with him in his house, drank tea and talked with him about Jesus. I gave him a New Testament and the Jesus Film in the Chechen language. He was so impressed that Christians had taken their time and money to translate the Bible and a film into their language that he shared it with several of his mullah friends.

I pray for Aslanbek, one of our Chechen guards who was with us from the very beginning. He was a kind and sincere man, the father of three daughters. One day he made the comment to me— "David, it is clear to me that your religion is real. I know this because you and your friends come here to help us by choice, not force. Islam requires me to do things but my heart is not in them. Your religion is true love."

I pray for Ramzan, a little Russian orphan boy, who lived in the streets of Grozny. In fact, he lived in the heart of Grozny, the Central Bazaar, a bustling, muddy maze of shifty produce traders, arms dealers and other war merchants. He survived on the scraps of the meat and vegetable stands. At 8 years old he was brought to Lamb's Home by an old Chechen man who had compassion on him. Through love and care from our Chechen staff, Ramzan grew up to be a decent young boy. Most of all, through the influence of our Christian witness, Ramzan had begun to teach himself English by using the Bible we brought him.

I pray for Esama, the little girl who understood the story of Zacchaeus. There is no doubt in my mind that Esama received the gospel into her heart and of all the children, she showed true signs of a soft heart towards Jesus Christ.

I pray for Hizir, Idris' brother. Hizir helped manage many parts of our Lamb's Home operation from the earliest days. He was always asking questions about our faith, and many times would agree that Jesus was more than just a good man and a prophet as his Koran stated. Even so, I never heard him agree that Jesus was the Son of God.

I pray for Idris. Along with his wife Maleka, they were the primary family that helped manage Lamb's Home and the Maleka Child and Family to Family projects. Idris was self-confident and brash. Like Jacob in the Old Testament and Peter in the New, he was a Chechen man with tremendous pride, determination, and fire. Having friends within the Russian military and the local Chechen government, Idris arranged all of our travel, security, and meetings when we were in the Republic—in his case the term "fixer" was a title of honor.

Before Lamb's Home opened in early 2001, I remember sitting with Idris at a house in Ingushetia late one night, talking about Christianity and what it meant to follow Christ. Over a plate of boiled chicken and rice and bread we sat for hours discussing this topic. It was somewhere around three in the morning when he looked at me and said, "David, our people are religious but they don't have the kind of religion you and your friends from America have. It seems that you really do know God. I want to follow your God, I just don't know how. You must show me and my people how. The war we have endured for 7 years happened because we as a people have turned our backs on God. We are being punished by God for forsaking Him. You have brought God back to us. I have asked God to help me find him again and I have begun to read the Bible you gave me. When I read it I feel free inside. I only hope that I can follow him the way you do."

I pray for Maleka. When I first met Maleka, she and Idris were directing the Salvation Army program that was assisting Chechen refugees in Ingushetia. From the time we met, I felt her heart open to God's word and the gospel of Jesus Christ. Yet, her life was deeply influenced by folk Islam, (charms, religious superstitions, and Islamic black magic). This type of Islam is prevalent across the Northern Caucasus region.

Once Lamb's Home opened, Maleka began to ask more and more questions about the differences between Christianity and her religion. Many times Helen and I had the opportunity to share with her the reality of trusting Jesus Christ with the salvation of her soul. Before long, Maleka was agreeing and truly believed that Jesus had come into her heart. As time went by, she began to talk to the orphan children at Lamb's Home about God and Jesus Christ. At our summer camps she would gather the children to teach them a story from the Bible. During our Maleka's Child distributions, she would openly declare that the reason for the gifts were not just to supply material help, but that she hoped every woman would see the true love of God through our actions. She also began to read her Bible and ask questions about certain verses.

God seemed to give Maleka and I a special way of understanding each other, although we could speak very little of each others language. On one of the last trips we made to the Republic, Helen and I invited Maleka to join with us in private as we took communion together. She accepted. This showed me that God had truly done a work in her heart.

In the New Testament, it was the women like Mary, Martha, Mary Magdalene, Lydia, Dorcas—just name a few— that were some of the first converts to Christ. I believe that if Maleka continues to follow Christ she could be the trumpet to herald the gospel to her own people there in Chechnya.

And yes, I continue to pray for Nasan, the first little Chechen refugee who had captured my heart in that sanitarium in Nalchik. Little did I realize at the time that her eyes, like stones of shiny ebony, would be like a beacon that would draw me to so many others like her, children caught up in the unspeakable terror of the Chechen wars.

David and Esama

Epilogue

I had breakfast this morning with my good friend Bill. We discussed many events including some that have made their way into this book, and some that never will. Bill and his wife Gail were on our first IHF team into Chechnya in 1997. He joined me later on several other trips into the region and over the last fifteen years they have been close friends and have supported our family through many of the trials and victories of our missionary adventure.

It was fitting that today, as we drove home from the Oak Diner, that we would hear a special news BBC bulletin from Moscow. Russian President Vladimir Putin had just anointed warlord-in-chief Ramzan Kadyrov as the new President of Chechnya. Once the leader of Chechen rebels fighting against Moscow, Kadyrov had switched sides and became Moscow's top enforcer to rule over his own people.

At the writing of this book, it has been three years since his father, then Chechen Prime Minister Ahkmed Kadyrov, was assassinated by a bomb placed under his seat while attending a ceremony at a soccer stadium in Grozny. Many suspected the Russian FSB to be behind the plot, but many Chechens pointed to his son, Ramzan. After his father's death, Moscow scrambled to install Ramzan as his replacement as Prime Minister, believing him to be the only person to keep thousands of former rebels under control.

This strong-arm tactic, exercised by men under his control while Prime Minister, has reportedly led to thousands of young Chechen men disappearing without a trace. This and other accusations of human rights abuses make him a highly controversial leader. May God have mercy on Chechnya.

In our final days of traveling into Chechnya, there were several times when we were interrogated by those we believed to be his agents, although we could never really confirm who they were working for. Things are this way in Chechnya—gray. Knowing we were coming from America and supporting Lamb's Home, we were soft targets for any number of people who made kidnapping for ransom their private industry. By God's grace and by angelic intervention we were delivered from this fate on several occasions that we know of.

Some have questioned my spiritual bravery and wondered why I didn't stick it out, maybe even become a martyr there. Others have questioned my sanity and said that I stayed too long. I wrestle with both opinions, and I can't answer either. What I do know is, for ten years God held me as a hostage of love to the Chechen people. As God's messenger of mercy, I was transported and protected from dangers seen and unseen, in a war zone where few in the world, Christian or non-Christian cared about, much less dared to go.

Through the grace of God I was allowed, along with faithful team members, to touch and be touched by literally thousands of war refugee families, orphans and widows—casualties of a brutal war that ripped out the soul of a entire generation of Chechen people.

We had obeyed God's call to go, and we had obeyed His call to leave. Now God is leading me to help share the Gospel with Muslims in other parts of the world.

- Yet, in my heart there is No Escape From Grozny.

Appendix A

Why Minister Among Muslims?

An American Christian reaching out to Muslims in a post 9 /11 world is just as radical as Jesus going to Samaria or the Apostle Paul being sent to the Gentiles in the early church. But didn't Jesus say go into "all" the world and preach the gospel? If that is true then I must go and share Jesus with the sons of Abraham, his older son, Ishmael's kids.

As Jesus said He needed to go through Samaria, I too, must go through the Samarias of this world. For the past 9 years it has Chechnya, Iran, Turkey, and Kosovo, to the side of the aisle that claims to worship the same God I do.

Some have asked, Why Chechnya? Why Muslims, aren't we at war with them? How can we love someone who has vowed to destroy our way of life? Going into Islamic countries is dangerous. Many of these people groups are embroiled in civil and ethnic wars. They seem to hate each other. Why then should we love them? I would love to support your ministry if you were going to France or Germany, but Chechnya?

I grew up in Alabama during the civil rights movement. Although I was a young child, I still remember George Wallace on the steps of the University of Alabama blocking the black students from enrolling at the school. I remember my first day of class when black students were bussed into our North Highlands Elementary school, just outside of Birmingham. I still remember my dad's face as they arrived to the shouts and screams of white parents protesting the bussing of black children to our white school. The wrinkles in his forehead are still vivid. I remember thinking, "My dad is a pastor, why is he so worried about black children coming to our school?" We sing in Sunday school,

> *Jesus loves all the little children,*
> *all the children of the world,*
> *red and yellow black and white*
> *they are precious in His sight*

—shouldn't they go to school too? I don't fault my father for this; it was a time of change and growth for lots of individuals as it was for America.

I remember hearing about a man named Martin Luther King, Jr. He was a black man that led people on marches across bridges in Selma, and onto the state capital of Montgomery. He also claimed to be a pastor. What puzzled me was that if we were all Christians, why weren't there any blacks in our church and why weren't there any whites in theirs? I was too young to know, but for the first time I was seeing one of the ugliest results of the fall of man.

Having traveled and worked throughout the world the last 20 years, I have seen this repeated many times. This hideous sin has raised its ugly head more times than I care to admit. It is the sin of religious racism. Ethnic hatred, Ishmael and Isaac, Muslims against Christians, the Crusades, Turks and Kurds, the Jewish Holocaust, America's Civil war, Africa's Tutsis and Hutus, Kosovo and Serbia, Kashmir and India, Iranians and Iraqis, just to name a few of the people that have suffered and inflicted suffering on their own fellow man. Human beings, killing human beings created in the image of God just like them, the same red blood flowing through their veins.

Sadly, the perpetrators have initiated their actions on a belief that their cause was religiously just, even holy. Their motives guided by a mandate of cleansing the land of the infidels and bringing about liberation… a better way of life for those conquered. After working in the aftermath of some of the recent ethnic conflicts of the 20th century, I have come to the conclusion that wars and armed conflicts only replace one ethnic group with another, thus bringing its own religion to replace the one that was removed. Truly, Ishmael is a wild man and his hand is against his brother's, but he is not unreachable. Jesus died for his sins too.

As a Christian, I am not at war with Muslims. They are not my enemy. Most of the people in these Muslims countries are ethnic believers, Muslim in name only but very few actually practicing their faith. They are created in the same image of God that I am. Some are seeking God, most are not. To those Jesus has commanded me to go and tell them how to find Him. We all need a Savior. Religion tells me to hate him who hates me, to take revenge on the one who threatens me, eye for eye, tooth for tooth. This same religious racism I saw growing up in Alabama, I see today. Maybe God exposed me to these issues of injustice and hatred when I was young so it would help me to see through it now, freeing me to obey His call to reach out to the Muslims, loving them into the kingdom of God. I am not on a holy crusade to convert every Muslim to Christ. But I do want to see Ishmael's sons come into the kingdom of God.

In the Bible, there are many interesting things said about Abrams son Ishmael. In Genesis 16: 11, Jesus told Hagar what to name him, Jesus himself gave Ishmael his name, "God Hears" Backing up a couple of scriptures, Jesus appeared to Hagar in the wilderness and promised her that He had heard her cries and that Ishmael would be a blessed nation and that many prosperous nations would come from him. Ishmael also was marked in his flesh with the sign of God's covenant just like his father Abram, his brother Isaac, and all the other servants of Abrams household, including the Jews of Jesus day. Genesis 17:23, this tradition, is still practiced today among most faithful Muslims. The nations that are Ishmael's descendants are Gentile, not Jewish. So, Paul declares in Colossians, there is neither Greek (Gentile) nor Jew in the body of Christ. We are all equal and welcomed into God's family.

In John chapter 4 we see the record of Jesus at Jacob's well. He was speaking to a Samaritan woman. The Samaritans were the Jew's most hated race, half-breeds, unclean traitors to the true faith of Israel. Jews walked around Samaria so as not to defile themselves with the dirt of this land. They lived on the wrong side of the tracks and prayed to a different god than the Jews. In their conversation, Jesus goes to the heart of the issue on religion and who God is. The woman tried to establish that they worshiped God in the mountain that her fathers had worshipped. The location was different from where the Jews worshipped. Jesus told her plainly that although she was very sincere, she didn't know who or what she was worshipping. After her encounter with the true Christ her eyes were open.

It reminds me of millions of Muslims who sincerely are seeking God, they just don't know who the true God is or where they are to worship him. Mecca or Jerusalem, it is not the issue. God can and wants to be known by his children everywhere but unless someone goes to the proverbial well in Samaria, how will they hear or know. This is why in His last words, Jesus speaks to his disciples that they should go to Samaria as witnesses of the gospel of Jesus Christ. I wonder if he had this village still fresh in his memory. I view my desire to reach the Muslims the same as Jesus did in going into Samaria. I can also imagine the Apostle Paul having these same feelings and passions for the Gentiles in Corinth or Ephesus.

Not everyone shares my zeal. Some modern day disciples and teachers have become like James and John in wanting to call down fire from heaven to consume the village in Samaria when the people didn't receive Jesus. In fact, just days after 9/11, I was dumbfounded to hear this same attitude from a respectable pastor in my area as he made the statement in anger, "If the Muslims don't like our Christianity, then we should just nuke them and let them all go to hell"! Sounds like fire from heaven to me. I guess nothing is new under the sun.

I saw this same attitude at a pastor's conference in New York several years ago. It was just after the horrible hostage incident in Beslan, Northern Ossetia. A nationally known speaker and author spent hours informing the pastors of how dangerous the Jihadis' were and that we Christians in America better wake up and equip ourselves to combat the wave of Islamic terrorist or we might be facing something similar on our own soil. During a session break, he challenged me and asked if I thought working among Chechen terrorist would bring any Christian fruit, and wouldn't it be better if I would spend my resources and energies in some more fruitful place?

Biting my tongue, I walked out of the conference and never went back. My heart was grieved and I wrestled with every fiber in my being to keep quiet and to let it go. I wanted to say to him, "Were you there? Do you know what really happened? Do you personally know some of the people who died in that tragedy? Do you care enough to give your life and resources to go there and share the gospel so that these events might never happen again? If you did, you would spend as much time exhorting the Christians to share God's love towards Muslims as you do stirring them up to fear them. But that wouldn't sell books and tapes. And it sure wouldn't play well on the radio programs you use to dish out more brain candy to the choir who supports your opinion. I thank God that I didn't say this to him. It would only have hurt me more.

Acts 2:5-11 is the biblical compass to show God's great love to Muslims and the Middle East. The second chapter of Acts is usually referred to when pastors share about the Pentecostal experience of tongues or the great sermon Peter gave that brought thousands to Christ that day. For me, I am fascinated with the people groups present that day. A careful look will reveal the faces from Kurdistan, Iraq, Southern and Northern Caucasus, Judea, Turkey, Egypt, Libya, Cyrene, Italy, Crete, and finally Saudi Arabia—the true Arabs.

What an amazing thought—the birthplace of the church of Jesus Christ was first in Jerusalem, and then the entire Middle East. Most American Christians are uncomfortable to think that Abraham could have resembled Saddam Hussein in his younger years. After all, he was from Ur of the Chaldeas, or modern day Basra, in Southern Iraq. Some of the Bible's greatest Old Testament figures are buried in Iran, or ancient Persia. Queen Esther for one, King Cyrus, Daniel spent a lot of time in Iran. Recently, a friend from Iran was to visit the U.S.A. and he expressed concern to me about how Christians would receive him given the tensions between Iran and America. I told him to just tell the Christians he was from Persia and few would make the connection.

Imagine, the great Apostle Paul was born and raised in what we call Turkey today! Before he wrote most of the New Testament, he was the church's worst fear, killing and putting Christians in prison in the name of God! After his conversion, God took him back to the very place that he was first persecuting Christians, but this time, to prepare for missionary service. His first short term mission was to Damascus, Syria.

The one sad thing about this passage of scripture is that today, most of the nations listed here are now under the crescent moon of Islam. But that is the very thing that motivates me to carry the gospel to the Muslim world. God wants to see His kingdom come full circle and return to the very point of beginning—to the sons of Isaac and Ishmael.

Appendix B

Living Dangerously in the Hands of God

James Miller was a British journalist who died from an Israeli bullet in 2003 while filming a documentary covering effects on children caught in the middle of the Palestinian and Israeli conflict in Gaza. Daniel Pearl was brutally beheaded in Pakistan while covering the war on terror for the Wall Street Journal. Christian Science Monitor reporter Jill Carroll was kidnapped and held hostage for over three months in Baghdad, Iraq while telling the story of innocent Iraqis suffering through war and bloodshed.

Ali was a young Chechen reporter who independently wrote stories for Agency France Press during the war in Chechnya. He also helped IHF at our Lamb's Home facility from time to time. He was a nice young man with a wife and two children. We spent time together as friends. On July 4th 2003, he was kidnapped in the city of Nazran, Ingushetia never to be seen again.

All of these people had one thing in common. They believed in their cause…the world needed to hear their story…a story of what was happening to other people. They made a conscious choice to face the dangers and their personal fears for their cause.

For some, their risk cost them their life. They were modern day martyrs for their beliefs.

The story of David and Goliath in the Bible tells of a young man who lived out his faith in God against very real dangers. He boldly declares, "Is there not a cause!" Goliath was conquered because a young boy believed in His God, no matter what the dangers were.

Early church history is filled with stories of martyrs. Martyrdom is an extreme form of Christian witness, the act of giving your life as a final act of devotion to Jesus Christ.

In recent times, people have come to view religious martyrdom only in the context of Muslim extremism, and that is a tragic thing. In the Christian tradition, martyrdom is very different.

The first martyr for the faith was Jesus Christ. On a human level, he became embroiled in the religious and political controversies of His time. He could have slipped away to the Judean countryside and avoided or delayed His death on the cross, but He knew He had to give up His earthly life to fulfill His Father's greater plan.

Many early leaders of the Church gave up their lives as martyrs for their faith. Most were on missionary journeys to the far reaches of the world, and they too ran against political and religious forces that wanted to crush them. Stephen died at the hands of a mob (Acts 7), and according to church history Matthew was beheaded with an axe, Mark was dragged to pieces by the people of Alexandria, Egypt. Peter was crucified upside down and Paul was beheaded with a sword.

Many ordinary Christians suffered death at the hands of authorities for their faith in Christ. One of the poignant stories that comes down to us is that of Perpetua, who lived in Carthage in the third century. She was a young woman with a baby, and was taken hostage by Emperor Septimus Severus who held her as a common criminal until she renounced her faith. Even Perpetua's father tried to persuade her to deny Christ and embrace worship of the Emperor.

Perpetua was steadfast, however, and refused to deny her Lord. Here is an account of her final moments:

The young woman was brought to the executioner, at which time Perpetua called out to some grieving Christian friends, "Give out the word to the brothers and sisters; stand fast in the faith, love one another, and don't let suffering become a stumbling block to you." She was taken to the gladiator to be beheaded. . . . His first blow was not sufficient. Perpetua cried out in pain, and took the gladiator's trembling hand and directed the sword to her throat and it was over.

All Christians must ask themselves, "Am I willing to risk my life for God's cause? Am I willing to be taken hostage or die as a believer in Christ? Do I take God's command "Take the Gospel to all nations" seriously enough to go, even if it means dying there? We ask about the risk, and what our death for the cause of Christ might mean to our wives, children, parents and others.

This issue has been answered in my Christian experience over the last 20 years as the Lord has sent me to areas of the world that are dangerous and less traveled by most. I have followed the Lord's will as I understood it, but that doesn't mean that there haven't been times when I was afraid for my life.

I remember the sick feeling that gripped my gut upon hearing a sinister remark made by a Russian border guard. He said, "Oh, we have the six million dollar guest," referring to the black market value he could get for kidnapping me and two other foreigners as we crossed a military checkpoint in Chechnya. I was afraid.

In fact, every time I crossed into Chechnya to share the gospel I feared for my life and those with me. In a war zone there was always a chance that something terrible could happen. It was such a real possibility that I tried to prepare my own heart, and prepare my family, for this eventuality on every trip. It was dangerous, but if the Chechen people were to ever to learn about Jesus, it would be through those who went to share the love of Christ in word and deed.

I faced this issue before the Lord called me to Chechnya. I spent time in Kosovo at the height of the war between the Kosovo Liberation Army (KLA) and the Serbian militia. One day, on my way to visit a Kosovar refugee camp to share the gospel and bring humanitarian aid, I mistakenly took a wrong turn and found myself driving into a Serbian village. Out of nowhere, a hostile mob of young Serbian men began to throw rocks and rush towards my vehicle from the front and the back. I wondered what was going on. It then dawned on me--I had Albanian license plates on the front of the jeep! I called on the Lord for help.

Accelerating off the road and down a ditch, I was able to drive around the mob in front and then back up onto the road. In a cloud of dust, rocks, and grass flying- it all happened so fast. I was in danger, but God faithfully protected me.

There will be dangers in sharing the Gospel. That has already been determined. The issue is, do we believe in the cause enough, and do we love those who need to hear the story enough, to face our fears and live totally abandoned to God's call?

There were many martyrs in Chechnya, Christian and Muslim, Russian Orthodox, Chechen Jihadist. They all died for their cause. Some died by choice, most did not. Most died as innocent civilians. Men, women, children - all caught in the vicious meat grinder of war. Grozny, Chechnya's capital became an evil place—living up to it's literal translated meaning in the Russian language, "horrible," a place no one wanted to go. Some claimed that God had forsaken it, but I didn't think so. If He had, this story would have never happened.

I am not brave, nor am I a spiritual hero. I do not seek to be martyred, but following Jesus could lead to that. Either way, I want to follow Him where He leads, even dangerous areas. Whether to tranquil shores or war-torn countries, my faith comes down to obedience. That obedience and love for Christ continues to motivate me to share the gospel in Islamic areas of the world. I have counted the cost. It is worth it.

"Patres! Three weeks from now, I will be harvesting my crops. Imagine where you will be, and it will be so. Hold the line, stay with me. If you find yourself alone, riding in green fields with the sun on your face, do not be troubled. For you are in Elysium, and you're already dead! Brothers, what we do in life...echoes in eternity". Maximus – Russell Crowe - Gladiator

"I count all things loss...to gain Christ" The Apostle Paul-Philippians 3:17 Holy Bible

Contact Information

For Additional Copies of this book write to:

book@noescapefromgrozny.com